Architecture of the Possible

Tristan Garcia
with Jean-Marie Durand

Architecture of the Possible

Translated by Christopher RayAlexander,
Abigail RayAlexander, and Jon Cogburn

polity

Originally published in French as *L'architecture du possible* © Presses universitaires de France/Humensis, 2021

This English edition © Polity Press, 2022

Polity Press
65 Bridge Street
Cambridge CB2 1UR, UK

Polity Press
111 River Street
Hoboken, NJ 07030, USA

ISBN-13: 978-1-5095-5223-8
ISBN-13: 978-1-5095-5224-5 (paperback)

A catalogue record for this book is available from the British Library.

Library of Congress Control Number: 2022934666

Typeset in 11 on 14pt Sabon
by Cheshire Typesetting Ltd, Cuddington, Cheshire
Printed and bound in Great Britain by CPI Group (UK) Ltd, Croydon

The publisher has used its best endeavors to ensure that the URLs for external websites referred to in this book are correct and active at the time of going to press. However, the publisher has no responsibility for the websites and can make no guarantee that a site will remain live or that the content is or will remain appropriate.

Every effort has been made to trace all copyright holders, but if any have been overlooked the publisher will be pleased to include any necessary credits in any subsequent reprint or edition.

For further information on Polity, visit our website:
politybooks.com

Contents

LANGUAGE, THOUGHT, AND FICTION

Starting a conversation when you also want to avoid speaking in a way that's too direct or brutal is not a straightforward affair. While trying to strike a balance between discretion and eagerness, I would like to begin by considering your recent writings and asking you to do something that might be impossible, namely, to describe your writing style and the way that you use language as a material to craft thought and fiction.

Are "philosopher" and "writer" the same thing? How are (de)constructing theories and inventing characters similar, and how are they different? Moreover, why do you feel the need to take up both of those pursuits at the same time?

Because I grew up in a family that had books, what I wanted to make and what I learned how to make were books. From an early age, my passion was centered on the written word, and I put my energy into trying to recreate those printed objects, those bound sheets of paper. They seemed to contain the whole world in miniature. The secret of the universe seemed to lie between their covers, which my mother and father would sometimes wrap in greaseproof butcher's paper.

My environment is made of language in general and writing in particular. My personality took shape in these surroundings.

If I'd been raised in another environment, I might have had a similar character. I might have had the same worldview but expressed it in some other way. I don't have many other skills, but it seems to me that whether I'm writing, thinking, cooking, or even playing sports, I have the same strengths and weaknesses. What if I were a professional sports player? What if I were a cook? Even if these counterfactual thought experiments are illusory, they allow me to imagine reasonably well the possibility of different ways of being that aren't based on thinking of abstract concepts and characters or writing.

For me, philosophy and literature aren't absolutes. They are the surroundings in which I grew up, the environment where my dispositions were developed to varying degrees, with my family's encouragement and at school as well.

I feel like I live and breathe language and the images and ideas that are formed out of words. Another person might find this view abstract or abstruse. But, for me, this is a primordial, enveloping condition, like an amniotic fluid made of signs. Social interactions aren't always easy for me. I love meeting another person, a kindred spirit, and discussing things with them. However, in a group setting, I kind of switch off a bit. Sometimes, I have to push myself. I have to play a role, and that doesn't come naturally to me. After a long period of careful existence in the social realm, the abstractness of words brings me back to a reassuring place where I can, as we say, gather my thoughts, and rediscover the center of who I am. There, within the abstract forms of thought and language, I can breathe easy, I can find my way around, and the world regains an order that comforts me. The chaos of the world's sensations, desires, and contradictory forces isn't altogether banished. Nevertheless, word by word, it becomes a little more livable. I've done the same ever since I was a child, going over lists in my mind and classifying things as a means of organizing what I've perceived, heard, felt, seen, and read. It's like the experience of a child from the country who has to go to the big city every morning. There, the child is jolted by the sights and sounds and jostled by the rushing crowds. Then, when returning home and walking on a path deep in the woods, the child's steps are more assured. Even though that path would surely frighten other children, for this child, it's even and familiar. It's a place to find one's bearings, a place to breathe easy. This doesn't mean that the child no longer wants to go back to the city to play with its friends and discover the wide urban world. It just means that the child still needs to return regularly to its home, a sort of forest within – the protected place where the child grew up. It's there that it can stave off being spread too thin by necessities and obligations. That place also protects it from being dissolved within the infinite mass of all the things that remain to be discovered and explored. It's a refuge from the loves and hates that threaten to tear the child apart. It's a haven from both the intelligence and foolishness of its peers – and from the child's own intelligence and foolishness as well.

Language, my language, has always had this effect on me.

I reflect and write so that I can return to that place as often as possible.

This place that you speak of, is it one uniform space?

Gradually, as I left childhood behind, that familiar place of language divided in two for me.

It split like a cleft tongue. It makes me think of those mythical peoples of long ago who were imagined by medieval troubadours to have spoken the "language of the birds" with their forked tongues. Whether it was naturally divided in two or had been cut that way during a ritual initiation, that tongue was supposed to allow them to speak two languages at once.

One part of my mind's language remains attached to legendary stories and to fiction, to all of the tales that I told myself as a child, to all of the stories that were read to me before I went to sleep, and to a sort of lie as well, to illusions that – as I've since discovered – don't exist in reality, and to imagination in general.

During my adolescence, another part of my language became more attached to ideas rather than to images. This part has a stronger connection to abstractions, general features, the laws of the world, and a kind of scientific approach.

The first language is childlike, and, in my opinion, it seems to speak to the whole world. It's democratic. The second language developed during puberty and is shaped by scientific and political education, by the discovery of the real, by that which offers external resistance, by what there really is. This language enjoys disappointing rather than enchanting. It's a more constrained and aristocratic language. It's a language that's subject to

4

authorities. This language entails requirements governing its utterance, its rhetoric, and its truth. It has norms
and laws. It's the language of a young person who
makes friends, who then belongs to a generation, and
who wants to understand and change its world.

*You mentioned understanding the world, but also changing
it. Does each of these aspirations require a different kind
of story?*

The duality of the double language that developed
within me became increasingly pronounced. When I
began to publish, I thought it was important to respect
the clear separation within this language and clearly
separate my desire for stories from my desire for theory.

While growing up in France at the end of the twentieth century, I came to distrust heavily theoretical fiction
and overly poeticized philosophy. Those combinations
were very much in style at the time, but they no longer
suited me. That space tied my forked tongue up in
knots. During the 1990s, Heideggerian influence was
still very strong in French philosophy for my professors
and for the intellectuals of that period, in the same way
that Blanchot had become the overpowering authority in literary studies. It was like one of Rousseau's
thoughts from *Essay on the Origin of Languages* that
Derrida would later discuss: the philosopher was a poet,
and the poet was a philosopher. Unfortunately, the
philosopher was a failed poet, as we see in Nietzsche.
Derrida and some of his disciples seemed to exist in a
sort of muddled relationship with language, one that
didn't appeal to me. Double meanings, a charming
insistence on the central and almost exclusive power of

ambiguity in language, the constant evasive maneuvers (and the resulting impossibility of arguing a thesis), rhetorical cunning, the eclipsing of *realia* (real things) by *dicta* (spoken things), etc., all of that was very tedious for me. The world was no longer expressed or discussed. I tried to read Nancy, Lacoue-Labarthe (whom I preferred, because he truly was a poet), and even Stiegler, but I always came out at the other end feeling cheated. Questions of value were always eclipsed by questions of meaning, and problems concerning definition were constantly dodged thanks to the continuous slippage of signification. I had the feeling that I was watching the elite of the philosophical word who conserved their power through their seductive and sophomoric scholarly mastery, but who never really had anything much to say. Any call for precision caused them to flee. When the time came to make a decision and reach a conclusion, they would sit on the fence. However, what they wanted more than anything else was to keep possession of the word by constantly batting it back and forth amongst themselves.

I would have to wait until I discovered Wittgenstein and the so-called Anglo-Saxon analytic tradition to find a philosophical language that had been freed from this poetic fixation. Quine was very important for me, as well as some of Austin's short essays and the metaphysics of Lewis, Armstrong, and Plantinga. I never joined that movement or its approach to metaphysics, but it helped me to move past French post-Heideggerian language.

Alongside your distrust of dominant philosophy, what position did you adopt regarding the literary tradition?

In an almost symmetrical way, what I disliked in literature was that constellation of authors that gravitated around autofiction. Instead of manifesting the full power of imagination, autofiction plays a game of hide-and-seek with the true self, meaning one's family history, biography, one's individual self-expression, etc.

I didn't want to take the imagination-motivated part of my language and turn it around on myself, to reach into my self and the experiences that I'd already lived in order to find the fabric for a literary kind of truth. I wanted to use language to be someone else, come to know other lives, take on other bodies, and disembody and reincarnate myself. More than anything else, I wanted to imprint those other lives within myself rather than externalize and express myself through others.

I was looking for a language that would separate me from my voice and that, above all, would not speak my truth.

For as long as possible, I've told myself that I would write books in a way that maintained a careful separation between my persona as a novelist and my persona as a philosopher.

This careful distinction between the novelist and the philosopher sounds like walking a tightrope. Was it easy to maintain?

The whole system is definitely a bit complicated, but I'm sure that we all construct ourselves in a similar way. There is within us something like a little system of weights, counterweights, and pulleys. Even if it happens unconsciously or implicitly, we imagine what we are and what we do with this kind of living machinery. We use that machinery to avoid having a lifeless conception of ourselves.

In order to feel alive, I need this balance or, better yet, this permanent imbalance, between my passion for stories and images on the one hand and my passion for ideas and theory on the other. When I try to describe or justify this situation, I ask myself this question: why do I so persistently run away from any confusion of or convergence between my two intellectual activities?

I remember that, in my youth, I detested the idea of self-certainty. I loathed those who seemed self-satisfied. I hated self-promoters whose every act and idea served to champion their own lives, which were spent with the primary aim of honing their self-image. That was one of those youthful fits of rage, the kind that usually stems from a fear of actually being one of those people that we reject and would like to banish as far away as possible from the core of our personality. I had an exaggerated disgust for any philosopher whose entire system seemed to me to be nothing more than a way to legitimize their own opinions, tastes, and ways of doing things. Such systems seemed to lend a universal form to a philosopher's unique and contingent personality and, above all, to their particular social class. I had no desire for a philosophy that would only serve to reassure me and tell me how right I was, and I had no interest in a literature that would only reflect my own ideas.

So, what could I do?

The problem went even deeper. I wanted to make works that mattered without mattering myself. I wanted to remove myself from the matter, to always be someone else and disperse myself as far and wide as my curiosity, discoveries, and efforts could reach.

I didn't want what I was thinking or writing to *reinforce* who I was. I almost wanted it to weaken me or tear me apart. Most importantly, I didn't want it to make me yet another strong individual among all the others. I hated that long period of the neoliberal demand upon individuals of my generation to "be yourself!" This was simultaneously an advertising slogan, a piece of self-help advice, and a moral imperative. I had absolutely no desire to be myself. What good would it do me? That's what I already was. Facing myself was really a matter for other people, since it was in their eyes that I was able to perceive what I was becoming. My role was instead to become attached to others, to everything except myself. And yet, that discourse about individual accomplishments and success was still there, telling me to become someone. That, I think, was what really filled me with dread: I definitely haven't ever wanted to become someone. I felt like I was experiencing something similar to the nightmares that Kafka sometimes mentioned in his *Diaries*. It was like I was being forced back into myself, as if I were an already-rigid corpse being stuffed into an old potato sack.

Is your attempt at maintaining a division in your writing something that your readers and the academic world understand?

My reluctance to present myself as an undivided, unified intellectual in a way that would make my novels, essays, and persona into a readily identifiable whole was a little tricky. No one could really understand where I was trying to go, the message that I wanted to convey, or what I was supposed to represent.

This put me in an awkward position during the 1990s and early 2000s, a moment when late capitalism still seemed triumphant. Whether through coaxing or as an authoritarian injunction, an individual was faced with the same demand: sculpt your own statue. Plotinus' old ideal had been taken up and industrialized. After all, as carefully maintained profiles on social media and dating sites indicate, everyone now knows all too well what they're supposed to do. They must be careful about how they present themselves to others, and they also have to become real entrepreneurs of the self by promoting their persona and what they do. In this way, each person becomes their own lifelong publicist. The language is familiar to us all: "That is so me"; "Thanks to so and so for their kind mention of me"; "At the heart of my work is my concern for . . ." Social networks have contributed significantly to creating this situation, but they didn't act alone. Since the 1970s, job availability has been decreasing in Western countries. This trend has resulted in a surging demand for individuals who wish to be competitive on the job market to spend all their energy not on working, but rather on selling themselves.

This is less a critique than a question of character. I never had a taste for the "game," for competitions where one had to show their worth and establish themselves by going up against and defeating others. Neither the literary "game" nor the philosophical "game" has ever been of any interest to me. I don't like playing any game that would require me to elbow my way in and present the most efficient version of myself to others.

Why do you think it is that you have no interest in such "games"?

It seems to me that building your own statue also means digging your own grave. By trying to win out over others in order to become someone, people end up working toward their own death. They end up building the tallest and most beautiful monument in preparation for their own tomb.

I've always thought that it's up to someone else to make me into someone. For a long time, I was paralyzed by the forms of self-presentation (like the very one in which I'm currently engaging!) to which one must become accustomed in scholarly and entrepreneurial circles. To present yourself, sell yourself, and find your place in the job market, you have to endlessly fine-tune your CV. During the years when I was searching for a university-level job, I failed again and again due to my clumsy self-presentation. My interviews were well known for being catastrophic. Even those who liked me would often sigh and tell me, "For crying out loud! You've got to work harder on your presentation." I was devastated by my total lack of ability. But still, in a very juvenile way, I felt like I was doomed before I'd even begun. They wanted me to define myself, and that would be the end of me.

It's very beautiful to never allow yourself to be defined and never be fixed in one form, leaving room for all future possibilities. Nevertheless, might you still be able to define yourself a little by fleshing out the meaning behind that total refusal of attribution?

How to remain a possibility? That was my obsession.

However, that's probably why I've wavered for so long between literary and philosophical writing. Maintaining my indecisiveness in this way let me also maintain the possibility and hope of remaining plural.

Whether I'm writing books, novels, or even essays, I know that I want to become different with each work, by any means necessary. I don't care much about making sure that my works have an overarching coherence. It often happens that people who've read and liked one of my books are bewildered or disappointed by something else that I've written. I'm now well accustomed to such disappointment, but it can still be a little concerning. People generally think of an author's work as monolithic. I certainly don't make things easy on my readers in that regard. Instead of feeding off of each other, my books are more like a litter of unruly puppies nipping at each other.

*　*　*

Because I've written and published considerably, I've thought about the possibility of using pseudonyms a number of times. I find that possibility appealing, but it also seems to me that maintaining multiple identities online is difficult, although I'm probably wrong about that.

I think that the authors from the Italian collective Wu Ming (which means "nobody" in Mandarin) have done a great job of creating a collective authorial figure through their novels. No one really knows which of them does what, and this allows them to reestablish a connection between their anonymized, collective creation and literature's oral origins. They reconnect with the Italian autonomous and Operaist (or Workerist) tradition's powerful political ideal of becoming "anybody" in order to evade the police, avoid being assigned an identity, thwart the state apparatus, etc. The same idea is also important for Agamben, and it also features prominently on the website for the publishing house *Quodlibet* (which means "whatever you like").

I didn't want to become "whomever you like." What I wanted was to be able to be a hundred people, each one of them different from the others.

In fact, every time that I had to promote one of my books, I felt a strong desire to disassociate myself from the very work that I was supposed to embody. I'd written the book in order to let it out, but in those moments, it felt like it was being forced back into the womb.

So I suppose that I was writing, and that I had chosen to write, books that varied so much in terms of subject matter, style, and genre that they didn't seem to have much of anything in common. I've written science fiction and sociological novels as well as books about ontology, identity politics, animal ethics, sports, TV shows, and formal logic, all in the hope of multiplying and losing myself.

* * *

Nevertheless, I gradually came to see that the naïve desire to not be somebody was close to a second desire that that period urged people to adopt. This desire was another liberal dream that took on the more ephemeral form of existing in a somewhat nomadic state, without attachments or origins. Anti-liberal reactionaries were quick to seize upon this idea. Philippe Muray critiqued this amorphous, virtual idea of a person in his articles and interviews, but he didn't push his argument any further. Long before this, Maurice Barrès's *Uprooted* had portrayed seven French youths who left the countryside for Paris and became modern men. Full of lofty plans, they lacked any connection to the soil and became uprooted (especially the Kantian philosopher).

Of course, it's also true that becoming many, multiplying yourself, juggling several different avatars, and moving between different jobs are all things that work nicely with the modern avant-garde artist's life on the front lines of liberalism's destruction. Self-artification is also a kind of laboratory where experiments are carried out in search of a new form of life. Instead of being a life you chose, it's a life imposed by demands to "move," "break free from the constraints of the past," "reinvent yourself," "become pure potential," and "never let yourself be reduced to your origins, your family, etc."

However, the reemergence of a decolonial and indigenist movement in France in the 2010s made me realize that this "desire to be multiple" could also be wielded against the dominated in order to dismantle the identities that are central to political activism. For example, it could be used strategically to encourage people to deny their Blackness, to discourage people from finding their ancestors within themselves to better understand how they've been racialized, or to prevent people from constructing an indigenous identity grounded in dignity and pride.

My desire to be a multitude and not have a fixed identity had to do with my status as a middle-class white man. My social identity tends to be what the society in which I live privileges and sees as neutral. This is something that we know instinctively. We don't need to learn the discourse of activism in school to understand this privilege.

Ralph Ellison's works like *Invisible Man* and James Baldwin's books allow us to understand the difference between an invisibility to which people are subjected, or the feeling of being nobody, and a privileged person's desire to become anonymous and multiple by refusing to be *reduced* to any one thing in particular.

And then, because we want to multiply ourselves, we also disperse ourselves. We risk becoming superficially adaptable as we repeatedly espouse the desire to be pure potential, to be thousands of people and take on thousands of faces – but, in terms of our current social context, we're also definitely somebody. That identity becomes like a blind spot, something that we would like to gloss over.

* * *

Even given all that, I still didn't want to entirely define myself based on my past, my origins, or my identity.

I often referred to myself as a "battlefield" in interviews in order to check the somewhat indulgent way in which I moved between theory and fiction and tried to be many, multiply myself, and avoid becoming "someone." I don't think that this analogy was very well received at the time. I was supposed to have multiple personalities to enrich myself without becoming schizophrenic.

Nevertheless, the truth is that there were times when I genuinely felt like my work was heading in that direction.

It's also true that my novels often give a tragic representation of the failure of certain theses that I've tried to argue in some of my essays. For example, *Mémoires de la jungle* [*Memories from the Jungle*] features the voice of an educated chimpanzee who both talks and behaves like a human. However, in the essay *Nous, animaux et humains. Actualité de Jeremy Bentham* [*We, Animals and Humans. Jeremy Bentham Today*], I was instead looking to reinscribe a line between the species. Ironically, the novels almost always expose the flaws in all of the ideas and truths that the philosopher tries to reach. Nevertheless, it doesn't end there. If the novels were to have the last word, my writing would seem to embrace a kind of perspectivism where each form of life has its own truth. However, in all of my philosophical texts, I try to defend a version of "common distinction," a kind of universal which is undeniably contradictory and yet still conceivable. Such universals don't hold up when they're placed within fictional stories. The novel defeats the universal.

This situation went from bad to worse. The further I got into writing *Laisser être et rendre puissant* [*Let Be and Make Powerful*], which is a book on ontology and metaphysics, the more I tried to defend a form of abstract thinking that neither feels nor suffers. On the other hand, when I worked on my epic novel *Histoire de la souffrance* [*History of Suffering*], I sank into a sensorial kind of storytelling, a writing of flesh, blood, and excrement.

For many years, I dreamed of no longer doing in-person interviews with journalists or critics. Instead, I wanted to make each of my books speak, with me as their ventriloquist. I wanted to act like I was a spokesperson for a novel or a philosophical essay about intensity, animality and humanity, we ourselves, etc. In that way, I hoped to no longer be limited by the pressure to be consistent. I would instead present myself as the battlefield where each of my books wages war with all the others. But that could only last for so long. Acting like I was merely hosting all of those contradictions turned out to be a sort of coyness. It was a minor manifestation of cowardice that left me pointing wherever the wind happened to be blowing. It was like I was trying to become a pure container of an idea and its opposite, behind which I could fade away.

Thanks to those around us, we get to know ourselves a little better as we grow older. I eventually realized that everything that I did still had a form and a face, and that that face was mine.

How would you describe the face that you saw? What do you look like as an author?

The problem remains. We have to imagine something close to what we ourselves are and present ourselves to others, but which image should we choose?

I remember that during a childhood trip to Rome, I was struck by the image of Janus, the two-faced god. Nevertheless, one does not have to have two faces to have duality. All faces are already a kind of duplication. The face that we present to the world is always symmetrical. It always has two sides.

Sometimes, I think that fiction and theory are the two halves of the face that I have in my professional life as an intellectual. In fact, most forms of life, including mammals like human beings, seem to be symmetrical. They're structured around an axis according to a bilateral or radial symmetry. Most of our organs are also arranged symmetrically. It seems a bit unnecessary to ask *why* this is the case. This is just how cells most often arrange themselves.

This may serve as a metaphor for the possibility that spiritual life is also symmetrically ordered. It may be that, like everyone else, I need an internal axis so that my thoughts can take on at least two different forms that mirror each other: the fictional and the theoretical, the literary and the philosophical, etc. But that's where the metaphor comes to a halt. It still doesn't quite work because literature and philosophy aren't parts of me. They aren't organs, not even symbolic ones.

* * *

A final image comes to mind, and it might be the best of all.

There are some amphibians that can move between different environments, like the land and the water or the water and the air.

That's it: literature and philosophy are like those environments.

I think that I would like to be a sort of amphibious subjectivity. That would definitely be my ideal form of life. I think that everyone else needs the same thing that I need: to be able to separate a particular environment from the rest of the world so that I can shift between different environments. I need for there to be two different practices that are sometimes complementary and sometimes conflicting. I have to be able to breathe in at least two different environments where I know how to get my bearings and survive. I need to be able to move between the realm of stories and the realm of ideas, or between the very palpable and the very abstract.

This idea is connected to a political ideal. It is, after all, the communist ideal as formulated by Engels and Marx in "The German Ideology":

> In communist society, where nobody has one exclusive sphere of activity but each can become accomplished in any branch they wish, society regulates the general production and thus makes it possible for me to do one thing today and another tomorrow, to hunt in the morning, fish in the afternoon, rear cattle in the evening, and criticize after dinner, just as I have a mind, without ever becoming hunter, fisher, shepherd, or critic.[1]

We should note that these aren't just hobbies, but rather practices and rigorous disciplines. We're talking about modes of existence in which one is wholly engaged and through which, or thanks to which, we completely comprehend the world in a way that differs according to the mode of engagement. This has nothing to do with the "uberized" ideal of a hyper-adaptable individual. It is instead a situation in which each person can fulfill their desired way of life. This allows them to become different beings with distinct practices. They thereby inhabit various universes with values that are so dissimilar that they often conflict with one another. After all, wouldn't the existence of Marx and Engels's after-dinner critic call into question the existence of the morning fisher or the afternoon livestock farmer, and vice versa?

---

[1] Adapted from Engels, Friedrich and Karl Marx. "The German Ideology," in *The Marx-Engels Reader*, 2nd edn., edited by Robert C. Tucker. New York: W. W. Norton, 1978. p. 160.

I just as wholeheartedly feel that I'm a being of stories and fiction and a being of abstractions and ideas. Those two sides clash on a regular basis. In certain moments, I can tell them apart and pass between them. That's when I feel like I'm really existing. I'm not trying to reconcile them, and I'm certainly not trying to conflate them. A bird isn't trying to merge the earth with the sky. It walks on the earth and flies in the sky. It doesn't reproach the earth for being too solid to support its flight or the air for being too insubstantial to bear its steps.

The same thing is true for me with regard to literature and philosophy. I try to live my intellectual life in two environments. I also think that this is an interesting way to model subjectivity if we want to avoid two of liberal capitalism's ideals. It keeps me from having to picture myself as "someone," a unique and compact Me that's determined to succeed and establish itself – this is the hard ideal of liberal capitalism. This model with two environments also prevents me from having to always be changing, free, and unattached, with thousands of possible forms – this is the soft, ephemeral version of the capitalist ideal.

I don't want to harden myself like a rock, to concentrate myself within my image, and to end up as a stony mask of myself. Nor do I have any desire to be potently volatile, like a thousand ever-changing, elusive personas all at once. I don't want to reinvent myself only to become empty and inconstant. What works for me is being an amphibious subjectivity that can pass from one expressive environment to another without ever becoming completely satisfied with itself or with what it does. The subjectivity that works for me is in perpetual opposition to something else.

PHILOSOPHICAL
FEELING

Why is it that metaphysics in particular attracts so much of your philosophical attention? To put it bluntly, what is it about abstract thought that you find so exciting? You often talk about it as a way of "accelerating" things. How can we grasp the meaning of this "acceleration"? Do you think that, without the work of thought, our lives would be lackluster, dull, or stagnant?

Engaging in philosophy, and especially metaphysics, means running the risk of simultaneously acquiring both an inferiority complex and a superiority complex. We learn to fight on both fronts: against the former complex, we have to become less guilty, and against the latter, less boastful. We have to carefully abstain from using any exalted or superior tone, and we have to avoid thinking of ourselves as the keepers of either absolute knowledge or knowledge of the absolute. We must not fancy ourselves to be contributors to what the Western tradition has dubbed the "queen of the sciences," nor should we claim to be the friends of wisdom, truth, etc. And we must also become accustomed to responding well to those who greet us with misunderstanding, mockery, and shrugged shoulders. I can already hear the remarks coming from the direction of the École normale supérieure: "Well, that's a bunch of hot air." Then, pantomiming someone blathering on with their hand, they would conclude, "This is nothing but idle talk blowing in the wind."

Reactions like that are precisely why I scrupulously try to avoid these three faults whenever I write philosophy: deceit, cowardice, and arrogance.

Let's talk about the first of those faults. What do you mean by "deceit"?

After high school, when I would talk about what I was doing or what I wanted to do, my friends who were going on to study math, social science, cognitive science, etc. would often take up that positivist critique that Carnap formulated so well. They would tell me that my problem was that I had no "area," by which they meant something like the kinds of "area of application" that you find in research. This initial assertion often led to a battery of further questions like "First of all, where are the limits of your field of study?" and "When it comes down to it, what are you really studying?" I would often trip over my words in response: "Everything? A little bit of everything? The being of things, or of all the things? What there is in a general sense?"

Of course, contemplating everything also means contemplating nothing. Admittedly, there's the option of cloaking yourself in a critique of the modern specialization of knowledge and claiming that a lofty philosophical perspective is necessary to study all areas. Nevertheless, this position quickly culminates in an empirical kind of knowledge that's honestly far too weak. It's true that readings that are always too hurried and introductory classes that give an overview of a field sometimes allow us to glean some superficial knowledge. It's not that hard to reach a basic undergraduate level of understanding of cosmology, linguistics, medicine, cognitive science, etc. But we can never cover all of the fields, and the more we cover, the more thinly stretched and superficial our knowledge becomes.

So, it's not really true that the philosopher's (and especially the metaphysician's) research area is *everything* or *every thing*. Here, we catch a glimpse of the deceit that I mentioned. It consists of trying to pass off an extremely superficial knowledge in all areas as a secret depth of knowledge. This kind of sleight of hand is commonly seen in the French Republic's culture. It's learned in French prep schools that focus on the humanities and are required for admission to the most prestigious French universities' philosophy programs. In these prep schools, students learn to adorn their rhetoric with the same old quotes from Nietzsche, Valéry, and Wilde. I didn't want to be the kind of thinker who's often a member of high society and who specializes in turning things on their heads by making the superficial seem profound. Just as they conceal doubt with an answer for every question, they likewise conceal their limitless pretension with false modesty.

Their last bastion of retreat is often located when they've just finished or are still working on their dissertation. That's when they learn that they can always hide behind the history of philosophy in order to at least exhibit their proficiency. This lends them a certain air of authority grounded in texts and tradition. However, it also signals the loss of something of the initial risk inherent to philosophy, and we mourn that loss.

What is that philosophical risk?

Philosophers and metaphysicians are often reproached for saying anything and everything, or, more precisely, for talking about anything and everything, no matter what it is, even if it seems nonsensical. The problem with "anything and everything" lies in its indeterminacy: it can be this, or that, or something else altogether. It doesn't really seem to matter. "Anything and everything" is everything and the opposite of everything. If we want to think of it as a metaphysical principle, then it's the infinite and indefinite Greek *apeiron*. To put it more harshly, this philosophical "anything and everything" can seem like the primordial cosmic soup.

And yet, my field is neither indeterminate nor an undefined absolute (and I think this is the case for all metaphysicians). I've never believed in anything like an ontological ground rooted in indeterminacy, or a Schellingian *Grund*, or a pre-individual given. No, my field is actually *the final limit just before such an indeterminacy*.

To me, metaphysics has always seemed like a form of cartography that can appear somewhat dangerous but that's also like an adventure in thought to the limits of indeterminacy. It allows us to travel right to the edge of "anything and everything" without falling in. This is only possible after we have completely – or almost completely – abandoned all principles, rules, and laws.

This is my area of study: the minimal determination of things, that which they have to be in order to be something instead of vaguely being everything or nothing.

So, what really interests me, the thing that I find fascinating in philosophy, and metaphysics in particular, is the edge of the abyss of thought. I don't mean the abyss itself, just the edge. Anytime I feel that edge, I know that I've found my "area."

This is also why I find this discipline so exciting. Every time I dive back into metaphysics, I get the exhilarating feeling that I'm taking off on an adventure to the unstable frontier of indeterminacy. This is a place where thinking is no longer protected by the principles of economy or the law of noncontradiction. In this place, it's like this, but it could also be something else, and it might even be the complete opposite.

Nevertheless, that doesn't resolve everything.

You mean the second fault, right? Is cowardice the problem that's still unresolved here?

Yes, especially when I'm around my politically minded and activist friends, the second thing that I've always tried to avoid is a kind of cowardice, avoidance, or disengagement. After all, metaphysicians try to describe "the world" in general, the way that being is structured at the limits of indeterminacy, as if there were an objective or neutral way of doing that. But when has that ever been possible? Why should I hide my position and my interests? Why should I cover over all of those determining factors? It's true that I'm a white man from a certain social class. I know about the position from which I speak, my familial privilege (which gives me a kind of cultural, but not economic, capital), the things that've made my educational background possible, as well as the things that've led me to have a taste for the abstract. I know this isn't coincidental. So, what's the point of acting like it's possible, from that point of view, to describe a world that's common to us all, even though we can all see that worldview tearing apart before our eyes? Why should I retreat from a war that's still underway? Why shouldn't I instead reinforce the side that I claim is mine? Wouldn't *not* doing so be kind of like aiding the enemy?

What's the point of that? You claim to be on the side of emancipation, and you call revolutionaries, independents, feminists, anti-classists, anti-capitalists, anti-fascists, etc. your comrades. In the end, though, you remain undecided. Instead of saying who's right and who's wrong, you say that there's some truth to everyone's argument. But isn't there a difference between being a revolutionary and being a fascist? Do you really see no difference between feminists and masculinists? Aren't you supposed to be fighting for good and against evil? You make compromises, you don't hold your position, and you don't speak up for your views. So, what's the point of thinking about all things if you end up saying that nothing is really anything? Is everything all the same to you? What is it about your way of seeing things that makes everything seem equal? What about suffering, injustice, villainy, and dignity? How do you plan on thinking about the being of all beings without judgment – and to what end? We all live somewhere. So what's the point of thinking from the vantage point of an immense metaphysical nowhere? What's more, in this nowhere, the necessity of immediate action for and alongside our comrades seems to become increasingly distant and fade away until it vanishes.

What's always interested me about philosophy is precisely the effort that it takes to extract ourselves – albeit only partially – from our determining factors, from the sides that we take and our positions, in order to observe our prisons from the outside.

To observe our prisons from the outside? Isn't that more a sociological rather than a philosophical pursuit?

If we really want to continue with that metaphor, it seems to me that the social sciences describe our prison from the inside. They teach us about the structure of the eminently concrete walls of institutions and conventions, as well as the floor and ceiling of our symbolic systems. The social sciences tell us about what holds us back, what restricts and constrains us by drawing upon the prison-like aspects of social experiences among individuals and groups. As we can see in many of the more furious writings of Bourdieu (who himself abandoned philosophy for sociology), this is why philosophy seems like a careless and vain field of knowledge that claims to describe social formation from the outside. From this angle, it looks like philosophy relies upon an illusory and misleading freedom, the kind held by a sovereign individual who floats along, suspended in the air of ideas.

Some people who dislike philosophy find it not just useless but also misleading. For them, what makes philosophy so unbearable is the fact that many philosophical texts make the quixotic claim to be able to free people from their imprisonment within themselves or within their condition and to deliver them to some truth, their free will, some version of the universal, etc.

However, this is just a *simulation* of ecstasy. It's nothing more than an "as-if" scenario. Admittedly, philosophy often develops out of ritual practices, orphic rites, Vedic ceremonies, etc. These often entail ecstatic, out-of-body experiences and mystical visions that give people the feeling that they're extracted from themselves. Even though this is the case, philosophy itself isn't ecstatic. Philosophical method is really a symbolic extraction. It's abstraction. It only appears to be.

Reproaching metaphysicians for describing the world from outside of their own point of view or for abstracting from their conditions is like chastising a novelist for making up Anna Karenina's thoughts. Of course they're made up! She doesn't exist! The novelist makes her exist. Metaphysics is a construction, or, better yet, a reconstruction of the world we have in common, the world we share, through a simulation of ecstasy.

With regard to the fault of cowardice and the critique of producing a kind of thinking that's uninvolved and disengaged from everything else, I would respond by taking care to remove myself from my position of engagement and to act *as if* I'd moved outside of what I, myself, am, in order to reconstruct something like a common being, something that might temporarily stand for everyone and everything. I aim at an ecstatic reconstruction of what keeps us locked up in our conditions, in our time and matter, amongst the living, within our subjectivity, situation, class, etc. And I remind myself that this certainly doesn't liberate anyone. Nevertheless, it does allow us to get an idea of all constraints from a point of view that posits the possible absence of the constraint of having a point of view. That's it, and it's not nothing.

And what about the third fault? You said that it had to do with arrogance. How should one understand what's at stake with that arrogance?

Arrogance has long been attributed to both philosophy and its professors, the ones who know. Worse still, they lecture us about how what they really know is that they know nothing. This paradoxically allows them to simultaneously have an answer for everything and to say nothing at all. When philosophers praise meticulous skepticism, they fuel people's modern-day mockery of such "wisdom."

Especially in France, the social status of philosophers allows them to give their opinion on all events despite their lack of expertise. They tend to conceal their own opinions when doing so. Philosophers enjoy vaguely discussing everything everywhere and at every time.

Why is this the case? When explaining the world, or their world, philosophers can lay bare certain things that other people can't see because their viewpoint is restricted by their interests or absorbed by their struggles. Even if they fail to grasp every detail and miss some of the quibbling details within each confrontation, philosophers claim to have a bird's-eye view that allows them to reveal the truth that lies beneath reality. They're the ones who can remove themselves from events, acts, and isolated individuals in order to abstract their substance or structure. Because they float above each faction, they can describe the battlefield as a whole. And people listen to them because they're supposed to have an authority based on their claim to give everyone else the general form of our experiences, which would otherwise be conflicted, partisan, and torn apart.

In this way, philosophers are called upon to be something like augurs. With a few references and sometimes a little jargon, they're asked to describe the general architecture of our reality with statements that begin with phrases like the following: "We live in a time in which ..."; "This is the age of ..."; "We are living through a crisis of ..."

Whenever philosophers talk about "what's going on," I immediately think to myself that I would do best to not listen to what follows very closely. It may even be best to distrust it. Only those who have some kind of positive knowledge of what exists can really talk about what there really is.

Of course, philosophers are familiar with the history of philosophy. They have a cursory understanding of all sorts of different areas. They can exhibit a smattering of historical awareness, enough literary knowledge to show their classical leanings, sufficient familiarity with cinema and television to include those with more contemporary tastes, and, when necessary, a few scientific notions that they've transformed from concepts into metaphors. Nevertheless, none of those things qualify philosophers to say anything accurate, true, precise, or intelligent. That is, unless they have an unreliable intuition about what's happening concretely right then and there. Someone who specializes in a certain area (in the present or the past) will always know more about the architecture of reality than the philosopher.

However, there is a way around the charge of arrogance: there is also the possible. As long as they're equipped with their readings, a method, and an idea, philosophers can define what structures that which lies beyond or beneath what there is, according to *what there might be*. Philosophers are neither poets nor prophets. What they do know is simply the field and limits of a possibility. That possibility may be logical, legal, aesthetic, epistemological, etc. Philosophers specialize in the possible. And whenever we think that something is possible, then *there will be a price to pay*. This conditional structure of the possible under a specific set of conditions is all that honest philosophers purport to know.

And that's precisely my goal: the architecture of the possible.

So, making the architecture of the possible your goal is what lets you avoid the three faults that you've mentioned?

Every time those faults rear back up, I remind myself that I have an area of study, a method, and an object. Those things explain the feelings of excitement, joy, and power that I experience whenever I do philosophy. There's a kind of vertigo that comes from making the limits of the determination of beings into one's area of study. Engaging with those limits always entails the danger of falling into indeterminacy and a fraudulent way of thinking. It's the ecstasy of acting "as if" it were possible to extricate or abstract myself from my own personal, familial, and social determinations as well as from my culture, my moment in history, and my language, all in order to reconstruct the world that we have in common from the outside. Nevertheless, acting "as if" this were possible always entails running the risk of actually believing in that possibility, which threatens to make me believe that I've truly been freed from all of my determining factors. That ecstasy is bound up with the wonder of seeing past the singular, particular determinations of what there is in the here and now to glimpse the architecture of *all that there could be*. That sight can lead one to the unfortunate end of being a professor who authoritatively declares what there really is or, even worse, what there should be.

The faults that I've mentioned restrain me, but I have to confess that the pleasure of the risk of thinking grows stronger each time. Sometimes I fail, and many of my works deserve to be criticized for venturing too far and too fast, while being insufficiently equipped. Nevertheless, I think that I've occasionally managed to extricate myself from my situation, to act "as if," and to remain at the limits of indeterminacy long enough to become a cartographer of our common condition and distinguish the architecture of what might be possible in that situation.

That's made me happy.

PHILOSOPHICAL ORIENTATION

Even in spite of all of the faults and limits that you've mentioned, you say that thinking has made you happy. From that we might suggest that it has a kind of usefulness for you, namely, that it makes a form of happiness possible. I would love to know what you think about this issue of utility, which is often a tricky question. What kind of usefulness can be linked to the exercise of thinking? Can and should thinking act as a compass to determine where we are today?

Some thoughts are more like maps, and others are more like compasses.

The ones that are like maps analyze and arrange our subjectivity's situation. Where are we now? What are the forces at work regarding different notions? Should we begin by drawing a line between constructivists and naturalists? Who do we find in the middle ground between them? Who believes in this concept of identity, and who will defend that other notion? What are we allowed to do, and what is forbidden? What is our field of possibilities? How is it constructed, and who constructed it this time? Who is this "we"? Who exactly are we talking about? I love working with these questions. It means reading a great deal, making classifications, and then grouping things according to their affinities; resemblances; genetic links; ways of being and/or doing things; epistemological, moral, and political positions, etc. Mapmaking is reassuring. Its primary effect on the mapmaker is the feeling of elevation and abstraction. Whether they want it or not, anyone who makes a map adopts the position of those who, in times past, would loom over battlefields from on high, observing from a cliff's overhang or hovering in a hot-air balloon. The contentment that these positions offer is captured in Lucretius' proverbial statement: *"suave mari magno."* Even if only for a moment, they can contemplate the others who are locked in battle while temporarily keeping themselves above the fray. They can chart the battle lines, just like I used to do when I would draw giant copies of Persian miniatures or the great battles illustrated in the *Mahabharata*.

This is intellectual mapmaking. This is the work of essayists – and journalists, most of the time. Nevertheless, this is often done shortsightedly, according to the crises of a particular year or decade. Because it's old and slow, philosophy is able to take the long view and observe tectonic movements that are often imperceptible within the interplay of intellectual forces. Philosophy can also locate the unexpected and distant cause of an earthquake that suddenly occurs in the here and now. It can do this because of its distance. From its vantage point, it can approach things from all possible angles. In addition to whatever real forces are involved, it also makes all possible forces confront one another. Philosophy imagines and anticipates. Moreover, as in the great Aristotelean doxographies, it also invents coherent concepts that might not yet have found their champion. Philosophy can handle an improbable possibility just as well as it handles history, and it can continue to do so right up to the moment when an improbable possibility becomes the current situation.

This distance functions whether we're trying to comprehend the evolution of our sentience in comparison to other animal species or our fascination with things like the collapse of a civilization dependent on thermal energy sources, the development of modes of production and labor, the degree to which violence exists within our societies, the objects of our aesthetic judgments, the way we conceptualize romantic relationships, the handling of death and the dead, the categories that we use to divide up the living, etc. The more that we distance ourselves from things, the better we grasp all the possible positions that we might take. The higher we climb, the more thoroughly we can map our current state and all that this state will allow us to do. Needless to say, the more that we think that our map is complete, the more we mistakenly believe that we've risen above it all, meaning that we also make ourselves powerless, as if we were simply spectators viewing things from the point of view of some far-flung star like Sirius. When thinking is mapmaking, it may well show us where we are, but it ultimately leaves us without any idea of where to go from there. Everything is open, too open.

In these moments, we call for strong, fast-acting "compass" thoughts to step in. We can carry these small but active thoughts in our pockets. They often only require the most minimal of maps: our friends are over here, our enemies are over there, these are the good ones and those the bad, etc. Thoughts like these allow us to focus all of our energy in a particular direction and set off right away. This kind of thinking has the distinct advantage of setting a course for us to take. It directs us toward a possibility that *must* be made real. This is what's referred to as a "line" in the language of party politics. Such a line is traced in the same way that ship captains once set their courses with a sextant and ascertained their position in relation to the stars.

This kind of course or line is made up of one or multiple values. Those values could be emancipation, autonomy, sovereignty, equality, a total rejection of authority, etc. They could also be social order, or the French Republican order. Or they could be an absolute prioritization of the decolonial struggle. Frequently, a course is an ordering of priorities. It can involve things that are more abstract, like the abolition of all borders or of all categories of knowledge. It could be a model, a form of life, a mode of existence, etc. It could also be the commons, or perhaps property instead. What about order, respect for hierarchy, national defense, or defense of the family? It could be the preservation of the past or the search for things like truth, a Baudelairean beauty that's always bizarre, the restless rushing of the sublime against endless iterations of ennui, etc.

Compass thinking promises to set a course that shows us where to go, a direction toward which we should orient ourselves as we traverse through all of our experiences and trials within a swirling welter of images, ideas, slogans, and injunctions. That's its power.

Is that power absolute?

No, certainly not. It remains unclear when it tries to tell us where we really are right now, in this very moment. It definitely isn't a map because it doesn't tell us what is close by or what is far away. It communicates none of the nuances of the terrain or of its elevation. It can't tell us where we might find a shortcut or a wise detour. Is there an impassable mountain ahead or an ocean in which we might drown? There's a strong chance that compass thinking might lead us astray. Its shortsightedness often makes us confuse localized tremors with large-scale upheavals and recent events with long-term trends, and vice versa.

In order to find our way, we need both thoughts that map the topography and thoughts that set a course. We need both maps and compasses. An analytical map is disorienting without a compass, and a compass-driven guide quickly leads us in circles or off a cliff if it doesn't also have a map.

Where would you situate yourselves between these two approaches? Are you more on the side of map thinking or compass thinking? Is it possible to link both approaches within a single, unified form of thinking?

Map thinking analyzes, classifies, and clarifies the details of a situation, a world, etc. However, it's also deceptive because its intellectual perspective simply flattens that which it lays out and thus lacks a horizon. It leaves its subject open to be explored from all directions, without orienting the exploration. I grew up with what was called "analytic philosophy." When I would finish reading many analytical works, I would frequently feel this disorientation.

Compass thinking, the kind of thinking that sets a course, is more messianic in style. German and French philosophy have often been critiqued for this approach. It emphatically fixes a direction or a purpose for existence, but it has little talent or taste for defining terms, describing things in fastidious detail, or analyzing the terrain.

I always try to map things out with concepts, right up to the point where it seems like the direction has been lost. At that point, I look for the most appropriate course. Then I return to the conceptual map to try to move forward and show a path to the reader. My books are structured like my thinking. They're like a hike through a mountain range of ideas. After having laid out the principal peaks, their ridges, the obstacles, and the possible places of passage, I look to see where we should go. Near which camp, alongside which value, and toward which idea should we aim? I then construct a range of examples, references, thought experiments, and debates among alternative options. When I arrange them all in opposition to one other, a dividing line appears. This is the path that leads toward a particular idea, value, side, etc.

I try to invent a different device for every work. I attempt to make a system of images and ideas to help bring the reader along with me as we move through a situation and meet back up with an idea. Whether or not they share that idea, I hope that the reader will have enough trust to take this walk with me and wait until the end before judging it. Did I take the right path? Was it the best one? Were there any others? Should I have taken more turns to the right or left? Or maybe we shouldn't have gone anywhere in the first place?

All I ever ask readers for is time, a little patience, and their trust. I hope that they'll wait until the end of the intellectual journey to decide whether or not it was worthwhile.

That's why I never try to clarify or be a guide from somewhere high above the readers. Doing so would strike me as a means of asserting my authority. Even if they feel as if they're lost, readers occupy their positions, which aren't the same as mine. They have every right to aim for another idea or ideal that's completely different than what I have in mind. But if they lend me their time and choose to trust me for a few hours, then, after walking with me, they'll know if they can take a path like mine to go from where they are to where they're going.

What I propose is neither a final truth nor a wisdom to be attained. I have no direction to impose or journey to require. All I have to offer is a partial map of our situation and our condition and a way of thinking that lets us move from one point to another. Readers are free to go wherever they want, from wherever they are.

But do you feel like most of us today lack the coordinates needed to orient ourselves? What do you think brings about that lack of orientation? Do you think it signals our departure from Modernity and our arrival in an uncertain time?

Whenever we try to orient ourselves through thinking, we discover at least two kinds of worlds (and two kinds of labyrinths): a liberal world and an authoritarian world. In Borges's short story "The Two Kings and the Two Labyrinths," the first king locks the second king into a labyrinth that's very narrow and complex. It takes him many years of searching before he finds the exit. This second king exacts his revenge by casting the first king into another sort of labyrinth. He abandons him in the middle of a desert.

This open, limitless space of the desert is akin to the liberal space. It has no limits, no borders, and no other apparent constraints. Everything is possible, and yet individuals feel powerless there. People no longer *meet* with anything, including resistance, and they're no longer able to leave. They're told that they're outside and free. They die from this arid, deserted freedom.

The first labyrinth seems impossible to escape because of its high walls, pitfalls, and long passageways leading to dead ends. That's what the authoritarian space is like. Nothing is possible any longer. You can only bang your head against the wall because there's a tight spot or deadlock around every corner. You're disciplined, compelled, and forced. People go around in circles and suffocate because they have to follow one singular delineated path that leads them nowhere.

Accordingly, any intellectual who endeavors to give some "coordinates" has to know the kind of space in which that orientation takes place. Is the labyrinth liberal or authoritarian? If it's a liberal labyrinth, then the best coordinates for thinking involve reconstructions. Paths can be sketched out, and limitations can be imagined anew. The walls and entrance must be found again. However, if we're dealing with an authoritarian labyrinth, then it's obviously a matter of tearing down the walls and finding the exit.

INTENSIFICATION, EXTENSION, BREAKING POINT

You've written a beautiful book, The Life Intense, *that lays out the genealogy of intensification and how it became a central idea for Modernity. Do you feel like your existence is intensified when you do philosophy?*

I really only ever use a single technique in philosophy, and it's always the same. Does it bring me a feeling of intensification? I doubt it. But it does at least make me feel like I'm intensifying ideas.

This technique results from a distortion and generalization of a distinction that's fundamental for ancient and medieval logic, and for modern logic as well. I'm referring to the distinction between the "extension" and "intension" of a concept. Intension normally has to do with the very definition of a concept. For example, we might say of a chair that it's "a piece of furniture with a backrest upon which one may sit." The extension of a concept is the set of objects that fit this definition. Of course, variations in the concept's extension will change in accordance with variations in its intension. If I only include pieces of furniture that have both a backrest and more than one leg, then I've added a further specification to my definition. From that point on, anything that I refer to as a chair must also have more than one leg.

The aim of my thinking is to understand intension, by which I mean the definition of a concept as a kind of *intensity*, which we might also think of as the variation of a force. When fewer objects are comprehended within a concept, they have more in common, and their community becomes enriched and more intense.

This is what happens with an inverse function: all things are such that an increase in extension decreases the intensity of their community.

In materials physics, there's something called a "stress rupture test" that's used in experiments to evaluate the resistance and elasticity of a material and determine when it will rupture. This reveals its *breaking point*.

This is what my thinking always does with regard to all ideas. I try to predict when an idea will reach its breaking point. However, I also want to see the point at which an idea becomes so concentrated within a limited extension that we present it as something grounded.

An idea is an inverse function that relates a given intensity to a given extension. By observing theoretical variations of this idea, I can open it up to more and more beings. In so doing, I decrease a bit of its intensity or, said otherwise, I take away some of the force that stems from what those beings have in common, or their commonality, as expressed in their definition.

We can take everything that circulates in our everyday and elevated languages and put it to the test. In this way, all of our ideas can undergo a stress rupture test. Say, for example, that you want to talk about "technique." Very well. You might then decide that "technique" belongs to humanity alone. But then you read a book by Benjamin Beck, an ethologist who inventoried hundreds of ways that nonhuman animals make and use tools, like how firebugs construct collective nests, how chimpanzees use fishing rods, how chickadees pry open caches of seeds with sticks, etc. So, what do you make of that? This is what always happens when we test these thoughts. We notice that those who try to limit the extension of a concept in order to preserve its intensity hide a circular reasoning behind their rhetoric. If we give some examples of nonhuman techniques, then our interlocutors will respond: "That's interesting, but those aren't *technically* techniques." Why not? Perhaps it will be because birds and chimpanzees don't use "meta-tools." When they talk about a "technique," they mean the usage not just of artifacts but also of tools and meta-tools, or tools used to make other tools. Nevertheless, there are also nonhuman meta-tools. Then, they'll further specify their thought: "We are actually referring to *lithic* meta-tools, which are made of stone. Furthermore, the stone must be *cut*." Now, this strikes me as a little suspicious. Why are such specifications necessary? Is this all just so that their definition directly corresponds to human activity? These people who would limit the extension of a concept first take a recognized human activity and extract a quality from it. Then, based on that quality that's supposedly proper to humans, they create a definition of "technique" that, in a circular fashion, allows for humans to be defined as technical creatures. In this way, we believe that we *recognize* technique. In fact, this is nothing more than a signal of our species *re-cognizing* itself in the hopes of objectively grounding itself in nature.

The same thing happens with all of the distinctive qualities that are supposed to be "proper to humanity," like consciousness, thought, laughter, etc. All of those qualities are subjective forms that stem from circular definitions, simply due to the fact that they aren't immediately recognizable. Subjectivity doesn't recognize subjectivity. It *re-cognizes* subjectivity. It decides the points or characteristics at which subjectivity stops. It seems to define subjectivity, but what it really defines is itself. It brings itself to a halt. Then it tries to find a characteristic that's common to whatever it re-cognizes so that it can make it into an idea or a concept. At that point it believes that it has found some proof of that concept's specificity. It uses that proof to classify and hierarchize things into species, genera, etc., and to both recognize things and rationalize what's recognized.

This is why I always begin testing an idea by resisting any ideas that claim to be grounded in a natural distinction or difference. Such ideas always conceal their own re-cognition behind the pretense of a grounded form of knowledge.

Nevertheless, we also have to resist thinking from the opposite direction. Rather than feigning their groundedness, some concepts appear so groundless that they seem to be able to be extended endlessly to match whatever rules or norms might be encountered. What do we mean by "art"? Whatever you want! Who perceives and who thinks? Not just humans, but the other animals as well. Even the trees and the vegetables can! Who knows? What about crystals too, as Ernst Haeckel thought? It all depends on our chosen definition.

But when we overextend a concept's definition, we push it to its breaking point. It's just as simple as that.

For example, we can generously affirm that everything thinks, and everything has a soul. However, this leads us to conflate thought or the idea of the soul with everything else. The concepts lose intensity. We expand the definition to cover so many differences that those internal differences become too significant. The internal differences between what does and does not have a soul or what does and does not think become more important than the external differences. This is how a concept reaches its breaking point.

What I seek is the theoretical point at which the concept breaks, the point beyond which it can be extended no further.

Between these two limits, i.e. extension up to the breaking point and a false groundedness, a space opens that allows us to dynamically vary and thereby test the intensity and extension of an idea. It's valid inasmuch as it's variable.

This is how my work has always been. It has been at the heart of my reasoning ever since I wrote my dissertation on the concept of "representation" and the modern difficulty of defining art. At that time, I placed two concepts in opposition. The first was the dissolution of the concept of art, based on ideas claiming that the concept of art is groundless, ephemeral, and dependent upon convention, institutions, and the varieties of aesthetic experiences. The second involved the false foundations of art grounded in European antiquity. This concept hinges on the belief that it's possible for us to arrive at such false foundations through rational deduction and then to hierarchize them. We see this in Kant's *Critique of Judgment*: by appealing to their form of expression, he arrives at the art of words, the art of gestures, the art of speech, etc. We also see this in Hegel's *Lectures on Aesthetics*: by intricately articulating symbolic, classical, and romantic periods, he shows a progressive spiritualization of matter.

The same thing happens when I write about the idea of "we" and political subjectivity. I try to simultaneously comprehend a number of movements. First, there's the way that collective subjectivity extends beyond humanity to other animal species, then to trees, the Earth, Gaia, the cosmos, etc., up to the point where the concept becomes inconsistent. Second, there's the reaction that makes subjectivities feel more intense as they join together into nations, families, groups, etc. Then, within these groups, they rediscover a critical understanding of their class and the construction of their gender, race, etc., and they thereby run the risk of thinking that they're grounded once again. This dynamic logic is what interests me. It's found between a stubborn refusal to be grounded and a critique of the breaking point where a concept has bitten off more than it can chew.

I'm against both the temptation of inscribing an essence in nature and the desire to extend or dissolve an idea and think of it as limitless and applicable to all contexts throughout history.

That's why my way of thinking philosophically is simple.

Simple? Could we clarify that simplicity?

Let's posit that we're interested in everything that is possible, and that we don't want to impose any other restrictions that might interfere with exploring whatever might be possible within the bounds of anything at all. In that case, I think that a philosopher can test all ideas and all concepts from science, culture, and everyday language by thinking about how they vary according to their extension and their intensity. Philosophers can investigate these ideas within the conditions of their historical moment and look for the point where they become so concentrated that they claim to "be grounded," at which point those ideas should be opposed. On the other hand, philosophers can also find the point where they extend, break down, and dissolve, at which point the ideas should be opposed yet again.

Philosophers make possibility possible. They make the possible determinate by endeavoring to define things and to delimit the intellectual and theoretical space in which ideas can function. In other words, they make ideas vary into ranges by either comprehending more and better – but with a common intensity that's a little less powerful – or instead becoming more intense, stronger, and more precise – but only at the price of decreased extension and a reduced field of application.

Did somebody say "fascist"? Let's test it. That calls for study so that we can take into account both the history and current usage of the concept as well as its effects and consequences. If we want an idea of fascism that's neither too limited nor too broad, where should that idea begin and end? Is someone talking about "force" or "violence"? Let's test those too. What about "collapse"? Let's test it out. What do we mean by "collapse"? *What* is collapsing? Some might say "the West," or maybe "Nature." The same method holds in all fields. For example, let's think about "music." Can it be any sound whatsoever once it has been perceived in a certain way? Or do we mean a particular kind of music, grounded exclusively in the Western tradition, with a specific conception of consonance that has been forcibly applied to all other human and animal musical traditions? We resist the moment when things become grounded, and we resist the moment when things hit their breaking point. As I understand it, that is when we philosophize.

Philosophical meaning is the meaning found in the elasticity of ideas, generalities, and abstractions. Philosophizing is an activity that both defines and participates. It's both analytic and synthetic. Philosophical meaning entails both a well-informed description and a firm decision. Of course, it's also up for debate, and it should always take account of the situation. It can be done in isolation, but then it has to justify itself collectively. We can't just stay in our corners and decide to label one thing this way and another that way. Social forces will resist this. The only way we can carefully test an idea is in a field where we thoroughly understand all of those forces.

This test also explains the feeling that I get from thinking. There's a sort of excitement brought on by producing constant variations, bringing an idea to its breaking point while resisting the temptation to ground it, and uprooting ideas that seemed firmly entrenched to make them dynamic.

That might seem too simple to some people. However, dating back to Socrates and Confucius, this strikes me as the governing principle of philosophical activity.

Doesn't this philosophical activity ever seem disappointing to you?

It may seem disappointing, but I think it's quite significant. It's an unending task that always has to be done again because the conditions are always changing. It's both exhausting and thrilling. It makes me feel a certain light-headedness, like an intoxication, because everything that I perceive and conceive seems dynamic. I envision all of the meanings produced by our species as if they were a system of abstractions and generalizations that are always on the verge of either becoming fixed and falsely grounded in nature – within the soil of "what there really is, objectively speaking" – or, instead, as if they're going to stretch too thin, become increasingly vague and inconsistent, and then break – because we act like an idea can be endlessly extended without becoming just a word devoid of meaning.

LITERATURE:
IDEAS IN A BODY

Does literature, on the other hand, strike a more sensitive and incarnate chord?

Literature clothes ideas.

Literature bundles up ideas for the winter. Many people think that literature strips things bare, exposes them, and rejects all that's superfluous. However, it seems to me that the opposite is true. Literature adds the superfluous things that truths, concepts, values, good and evil, etc. lack. While a butcher separates flesh from bone, literature instead returns the flesh to the bones of generalities. More than just the flesh, literature also regrows the muscles, nerves, flowing blood, sprouting hairs, secretions, fluids, etc. Like theory, literature too has an inert language made of words, phrases, and simple signs as its starting point. However, literature seeks the very thing that theory tries to leave behind, namely, what is here and now, what's happening just this once, in a unique moment. It's interested in the living, mortal, stirring, and fluttering things that can only ever be vaguely approximated.

When dressing up ideas both big and small, literature often starts by making them look ridiculous. Fiction is a point of view that permits the false to subvert what we think of as immutable, incontestable truths. This explains the importance of buffoonery in both drama and tragedy. It's important to make people laugh, and it's almost always impossible to do so with theory. When we theorize about what there is and what could or should be, we don't tend to joke around.

The idea that has most influenced my understanding of literature is the notion of adolescence in Lukács's *The Theory of the Novel*. There are a few paragraphs therein dedicated to souls that are either too narrow or too broad for the world (in the novel). Those that are too narrow are obstinate and closed-minded. Like Don Quixote or the good soldier Švejk, they limit themselves to an obsession. I love Ignatius from *A Confederacy of Dunces* because of those same characteristics. By contrast, souls that are too broad expect some great ideal to correspond to reality. Like Madame Bovary, they want too much and are never satisfied. When it comes to novels, good characters are really those that are simultaneously too narrow and too broad. In any event, they're ill-fitted for reality. The feeling of a novel emerges from these misalignments.

This is what made me fall for Donald Westlake's thieves and Robert Silverberg's tormented futuristic beings. The world wasn't made for them. They're like the square pegs that won't fit into the round, triangular, or star-shaped holes in a child's toy. They get stuck instead of passing through. This is the domain of the fictional: novels use a carefully orchestrated series of events to show how and why someone never fully fits within the world, or in fact, never fits in at all. They're blocked and don't fit into any hole. They may try, but, whether or not they want to fit, the result is always the same: there's nothing to be done because they simply don't belong. The easy response involves thinking that *these characters* are the ones that are misshapen. That approach leads in the direction of psychological literature that focuses on the askew, the accursed, and those who are labeled as "dysfunctional." However, the literature that I prefer believes and makes us believe that it is actually *the world* that's defective and ill-fitting.

Regardless of their literary-historical importance, the books that I prefer and the ones that I truly adore bring together a kind of narrative generosity, a child-ish and inexhaustible love of stories and exploring the world, a sensorial acuity, and the feeling that *something doesn't fit*. They give the impression that a subjectivity or a living body never really fits into the world. Some kind of game is afoot. There are so many examples I could mention of books that are funny or violent and that strive to make us see, hear, feel, and taste. In no particular order, these are the first examples that come to mind: Proust, Woolf, *Sentimental Education*, Stevenson's *The Master of Ballantrae*, Miquel de Palol's *The Garden of the Seven Twilights*, Joseph Roth, *Life and Fate*, *Absalom, Absalom!*, *Blood Meridian*, Robert Penn Warren, Gombrowicz, Céline, Giono, Flannery O'Connor, Donna Tartt, *The Rediscovery of Man*, Bradbury, Ursula Le Guin, Shirley Jackson, Stephen King, *The Gray House*, and *Vita Nostra*. I also love the

Epic of Gilgamesh, the Story of Sinuhe, the Icelandic sagas, the legend of Cú Chulainn, Amerindian stories, Chinese folklore, the *Ramayana*, and the Arthurian cycle. The European psychological novel isn't central to my fictional preferences. Unfortunately, we're taught in school that it's the alpha and omega of literature. It's just one province among others that I love, including mythological and epic forms of storytelling, as well as movies, comic books, and television series.

What do you see as fundamental to the form of a novel?

I look for a well-constructed narrative that's like a little house nestled in time that I can inhabit for a moment in my imagination. It lets me be in a place that's out of place, no longer has a place, or will never take place. I look for something that can be written but never solved. This something is more or less than a thought.

I also really like my literature to have something of a dark side. By this, I mean more than the simplistic affirmation that everything is permissible in a work of fiction. I'm talking about something else that happens in literature, an element that deforms everything that enters into it, just as the sun's rays are refracted when they pass through water. Values undergo the same sort of shift whenever they pass into fiction. They change course, and sometimes they are even contorted. If the good (if we want to call it that) is experienced in a completely naïve way within a work of fiction, it becomes bad. It's silly, dumb, or boring, and it makes us want to do bad things instead, just to try them out. Within stories, the beautiful, the real beauty of a face, a landscape, etc., is warped and seems uninteresting, dull, and sometimes even painfully contorted and ugly. If I call something in a story beautiful, it will no longer be beautiful at all. Then it becomes necessary to experiment with variations and find a way to bring that beauty back. How can this be done? That's the novelist's job. We have to start with something completely different. For example, Hugo takes ugliness itself as his starting point. In *The Man Who Laughs*, a young woman tells Gwynplaine that there are a thousand ways to be ugly, but there's only one way to be beautiful. In the same manner, what's monstrous in reality can be sublime in literature.

One can always fail at writing a novel. Much of it comes down to the artisan's technique. However, in my opinion, there's only one kind of error or fault to be avoided when it comes to the novel's project: we must not wish or believe that literature can convey the beautiful with beauty, the true with truth, or the good with goodness. Doing so would mean trusting in our good intentions, wanting to express truth directly, and putting our own worldview into a character's mouth. It would also mean treating readers like idiots by lecturing them on the world, life, and society. Above all, it means that we continue to act as though we're standing on the solid ground of reality even after having waded out into the waters of fiction. It's a formal flaw and a failure to understand the very essence of literature.

For this reason, whenever I write novels (successes and failures alike), my first mission is to destroy all the vestiges of my own philosophy. I start with others who are not me, and especially those whom I think are wrong. I take on their point of view. I try to feel as they feel and to feel along with them until doing so becomes unconscious. Then I tell their stories. I try to make it so that thoughts that initially seem false to me, when plunged into their bodies, can reemerge within a truth that's their own.

MODELS OF CONCISION AND MODELS OF PROFUSION

Can you name any models for authors who are simultaneously philosophers and novelists?

Should I say everything or should I say too little?

I'm still not sure, and it bothers me. Whether I'm writing fiction or theory, I constantly waver between two models: a model of concision and a model of profusion.

When it comes down to it, I love both. I love thinkers and artists who do too much and those who do just enough. I not only enjoy them, but I also want to follow and imitate them. My ambition is to elevate my ongoing work to the levels that theirs have reached.

The authors whom I personally see as models of profusion are the ones that come to mind when I have to think and write. I think of them whenever I begin a new book. That process is like diving into cold water, without hesitation; unencumbered by the superego; and with no fear of catching a cold, splashing others, or looking ridiculous. To name a few such authors in no particular order, I think of Hugo and Hegel, but also – and this might seem surprising – Stephen King's imaginary worlds, Silverberg's science fiction, Westlake's humor and crime fiction, Joyce Carol Oates, Tezuka, and even Prince in the musical realm. All of those mentioned share an abundant, flourishing output. Among their works, there's much that's good and bad, and also some things that are average. This is the result of an unstoppable productivity that seems to have a direct libidinal connection.

Who would be my models of concision? They're rare creators indeed. They're the ones who remove material. When they write and think, they cut out anything that isn't of use. Some moralists are like this. For example, in philosophy, Wittgenstein's work comes to mind, as well as Austin's articles, which are clear, dedicated to a well-defined problem, and seem to exhaustively examine a subject within a minimal amount of space. I also think of Lispector's elliptical short stories and Anscombe's brief, sharp texts.

A concise mind doesn't measure itself against everything there is. It doesn't seek to augment mass, and it's wary of anything that resembles verbal or cognitive diarrhea. It searches for what can be extracted from this flow. It looks for what withstands these currents and might be abstracted from them. It's interested in extricating something precise that stands in contrast to the blurry chaos encircling it. A concise mind tries to state things once and for all. It does so carefully and in opposition to the endless assault of disordered information. Once it's been stated, there's nothing else to say.

A profuse mind receives all tides and then makes its own waves. It offers no ascetic resistance. It's hungry. It is hunger. As Hugo said of Rabelais, it's a stomach. As an appetite, it's insatiable. It's also often jealous of the world. It wants to be the very world that surrounds it, but it also wants to be more and better than that world. It wants to be many worlds, an infinite number of universes. Hegelian dialectics seem like a machine made to ensnare all the productions of the mind, beginning with Socrates' thinking. Another profuse mind would be Whitehead, with his anti-dialectical prose and his byzantine catalogues of endless categories. When I was a child, I used to love this phrase from Baudelaire: "The universe is the size of his vast hunger." Strangely enough, I first saw that phrase on the cover of *Gullivore*, an ephemeral children's magazine. I think that that phrase offers a good definition of a profuse mind.

Incidentally, Baudelaire himself is concise, as in his *Fusées*, for example.

What are some possible models of concision and profusion in the field of theory?

When it comes to theory, models of concision usually take on one of two forms. They tend either toward aphorisms and dazzling poetic formulations or toward a simplicity, methodological clarity, and language borrowed from experimental science. They revolve around well-defined problems, theses, thought experiments, rigorous argumentation, and conclusions (even if they're just provisional). And then, without further ado, it's finished. They're polite to readers, as if they were guests. There's no need to bore them to tears with thousands of thousand-page works. Readers also have other things to do, so let's not take advantage of their patience. When writing philosophy, a concise mind distrusts style, which it views as useless and inappropriate pomp. For the concise mind, style just serves to mask the weaknesses and vacuousness of one's words through sleight of hand and ambiguity.

Early Wittgenstein is concise. So is Pascal, in his own way. Confucius is too, but Mencius is not. Dennett is authoritarian without being concise. Searle is clear, linear, and concise.

There are a hundred different ways to be concise. For example, I think that Donna Haraway is somehow both winding and concise. This combination matches her conception of the world as a living thing that's constantly transforming. Such a world is neither essentialist nor systematic. It refuses the kind of thinking that totalizes or ingests and digests beings, and this allows those beings to become something else.

As for other philosophical models, I also think that Fanon is concise, but this is because he's occasionally tempted by ellipses, poetic sentences, etc. After all, he also wrote poetry and theater. Eventually, catchphrases and political slogans entice him as well.

Thinking of the philosophers whom I've met and those who've been my professors, I would say that Alain Badiou is a model of profusion and that Quentin Meillassoux is a model of concision, even though they've both sought after some form of the infinite.

As for me, being concise first makes me feel a little thinned out, and then too meagre. After a while, I feel dried up and as though the world has been flattened. When experiencing the concision of authors like Pierre Michon, whose style is at once concise and baroque, or Jean Echenoz, whose writing becomes increasingly concise, I particularly admire their ability to purify language by first filtering out anything unnecessary, then anything ugly, and, finally, anything false. Nevertheless, I soon begin to miss all of the unnecessary, ugly, and false parts of the world. When being is made concise by an artist or thinker, the result seems too narrow and too tightly squeezed. I struggle to live, dream, or engage in sustained reflection there. It's too little and too good for everything that there really is.

The world is neither beautiful, nor true, nor good. It's also not the opposite of all those things. Because of this, when I choose concision and sharpness in style when writing and thinking, I lose the world's impurities, its mixture, along with all of its fatty bits.

By contrast, the kind of intellectual profusion that accompanies a love of everything in the world – including the high, the low, and the mediocre – stems from the frustration of having been reduced to a single point of view as one speaker expressing one vision of the world. Rather than asserting its objectivity, profusion is more about multiplying its subjectivity. It wants to say everything, but what matters most is doing so from all possible perspectives. For the profuse mind, nothing is ever enough.

Philosophical profusion draws on anything and everything. It jumps back and forth between disciplines in the hopes of discovering a secret passage that will let it move freely from aesthetics to metaphysics, from epistemology to morality, from politics to law, etc. I think that Vico exemplifies this. That movement is never far from falling into confusion. It tries to make a work or multiple works compete with a world or multiple worlds. Regardless of whether we do this with novels or philosophical treatises, we run the risk of overinflating and becoming *bloated*. Too much of making one claim after another, or of exploring one thing and its opposite, leads to an emptying of our thinking. Then it loses its consistency, disperses, and becomes scattered.

Concision has the advantage of being concentrated, and I long for that part of it. It avoids the more ridiculous aspects that Kierkegaard mocks in those who forget themselves and try to be everything. The more such thinkers attempt to make themselves disappear, the more awkwardly they stand out due to the farcically obstinate particularity of their existence, social position, and character. They try to pass themselves off as if they were the whole wide world, but they're really no more than what they are.

Concise minds are far more honest about this. They're open about the fact that their thoughts are just that – no more and no less than what they've chosen. Whenever the temptation arises to add something more or to reconsider everything from another angle, concise minds know how to stop themselves. They have a charming understanding of when to speak up and when to keep quiet.

These questions pertain to styles of thinking, but there's also more at stake.

I love both concise and profuse minds. I really can't choose between them. I would love to be like both of them or to be both at the same time, and that desire itself is probably the mark of a profuse mind. However, I also know that I can't be more than one of them and, in the end, I want to arrive at a decision, which seems more indicative of a concise mind.

CHILDHOOD AND IRENICISM

Having located ourselves between profusion and conci-sion, I would now like to move toward the question of your character and what might have shaped it during your childhood. Even if you're not so naïve as to believe that peace always prevails in either the world of ideas or the world at large, I've still heard you express your frequent astonishment that we can't find a way to get along in our lives in general. You're surprised that people continue to wage "war" on one another, spurred on by various motifs based on ideology, politics, aesthetics, ethics, etc. Where does that astonishment come from? Do you think that it has to do with an attachment to your childhood ideas? Is it tied to an idea of the world that your childhood allowed you to imagine?

Our different temperaments impact how we think. We might share the same system of values, subscribe to the same truths, and situate ourselves in the same camp, but we can still do everything in a different way. This is the *adverbial* part of thinking. Thinking can proceed slowly or quickly and gently or harshly. The adverbial part of thinking has nothing to do with its content. We can speak forcefully about weak ideas or intone the most powerful words in a weak way. Some people make all of their judgments as though they were warriors and act like authoritarians even when liberating others. That's just their temperament. I have more of an *irenic* temperament. It seeks reconciliation and refuses to see conflict as inevitable, as if it were the horizon that encircles our lives and the only way to achieve satisfaction or fulfillment is through struggle and opposition.

"Irenicism" comes from the Greek word for peace. Christian church history shows that many different dogmatic tendencies emerged in the early history of Christianity. Irenicism designated those people who worked to reconcile those groups by minimizing their contradictions and instead focusing on shared interests and perspectives they had in common.

I'm partial to irenicism. That's the way that I am, and there's nothing I can do about that.

And yet, it still makes me suspicious.

Nevertheless, deep down inside me and at the heart of all of the elaborate theoretical constructions that I put forward, I know that there's a desire to resolve or defuse conflict. Sometimes, the price for this desire entails blinding myself to a real war raging around me. Instead of taking a side, I would rather model my thinking on the battlefield. Doing so risks splitting my thinking into the two opposing sides as I try to understand the reasons and viewpoints of all the different belligerents.

I have no doubt that this way of creating and understanding the world of ideas comes from my childhood. It's how I remain faithful – albeit in a way that must be largely informed by retrospective fantasies – to the child who, at a certain age, wanted to reconcile the adults around him. I think that for many children, including myself as a child, this desire has something to do with the illusion that we're born completely new. We're like a fresh start born into an old world that's been torn to tatters. As we age, we too become just as ancient as the world. All throughout our lives, all we do is catch up with the age of the world. However, when we're little kids, we love to pit what we call our "innocence" and our newness against the history and society in which we've appeared. Almost every generation claims the privilege of having been born into a world that faces impending death, a world ruined by conflicts, depleted resources, exhausted ideas, and the failures of those who came before.

Because they were born, children think that they can put back together everything that's disjointed, dislocated, or decayed. Sometimes they're right. Much of historical change occurs thanks to generational renewal. In opposition to mortality and "being-toward-death," Hannah Arendt talks about "natality," the simple fact that new human subjectivities constantly emerge and make the world in which they've arrived a point of departure yet again.

In childhood, it takes time for us to learn that having been born doesn't make us an absolute *initium*. We continue the world and other lives that came before us. We are already highly determined by our situation, class, language, and heritage. Then the aging begins.

In adulthood, everything is inverted. It takes time for us to understand that other people have been born since our birth and that the world that we continue to inhabit has just started for them. We become just as stiff, uptight, entangled, and hard to change as the world itself.

However, for newborns, it's still possible to transform this impossibly rigid world.

Rightly or wrongly, I would guess that my irenicism stems from a prolonged, childish feeling of being newly born and untainted in a world at war with itself. This sentiment leads to the thought that a new or neutral perspective could make resolving our conflicts possible. I think this is why my works often seem to have a certain *tabula rasa* naïveté.

It would be silly if there was nothing more to it than this – just a childish idea espoused by the adult I am today. We're all born into situations permeated by interests and conflicts. If we remain unaware of that fact for a lengthy period of time, then we're privileged indeed. If I then continued to deny this fact, I would have to be either an idiot or a hypocrite.

Nevertheless, intellectual biographies can often be explained by a struggle within ourselves between the children and the adolescents we once were. We could say that, while the child that I once was wanted peace, the adolescent that I once was rolled his eyes and clearly saw that there was a war going on. The adolescent hates when people feign innocence. It disgusts him. He knows that peace is a lie.

At least, that's how I felt at the time. My Western generation grew up in an atmosphere that seemed to be generally peaceful, but that proved to be deceptive. Peace was presented as a well-established fact following World War II. At the same time, we were told that the remaining armed conflicts in our increasingly multilateral world were just lingering reminders of the chaos of the past. We felt sorry for the victims of the civil wars and the coups that happened in African states. We spoke with a kind of disbelief about Libyan hostages, Latin American guerillas, and Eritrean trench warfare. But then the little middle-class Europeans like me would hear their murmured message of the times: "In general," or "Globally speaking, you are at peace, and that peace will soon spread to everyone else, including the people of the Global South." This was the tale people told at the end of the twentieth century, and it was accompanied by a veritable aesthetic of peace. We joined in one big secular chorus and sang of peace and a world united in charity concerts: "We are the world, we are the children . . ." I remember learning in my European history classes about the lives of Robert Schuman and Jean Monnet, who are considered founding fathers of the European Union. We learned about the house where they solemnly planted the seed of a tree that stood for peace and liberty. I also remember that the notebooks at our school were decorated with the twelve stars of the European Economic Community. There were UNESCO children's books with illustrations of children of all colors united, holding hands, and smiling as they encircled the planet, depicting a better world. That world was already there or, at the very least, it was the world that we were working toward. The guns had fallen silent.

The more I poked my head outside and looked around, the more that message seemed to be false. Of course, it was steeped in good intentions. Nevertheless, when we constantly hear that "we are at peace" and then discover that we are (often unknowing) participants in thousands of wars both big and small, we end up feeling annoyed or angry at the idea of peace that they made us believe in.

Violent confrontations were presented to me as if they were almost invisible. The older I became, the harder it was to see anything but those clashes, all around me and at all times. I saw violence in the lives of people who weren't white like me and who lived in different neighborhoods. That violence was in the streets, but it was also in institutions with the strongest police presence. I gradually learned how to see the tensions and struggles that had been there for a long time. The actions, policies, and enforcement orders that the French state has issued in recent years are related to its growing reactionary rigidity in response to increasingly violent street protests. Nevertheless, that violence didn't materialize from nowhere. I'd once thought that the various means by which workers and bodies – both human and animal – are exploited, including sexual domination and neocolonial violence, were holes in the fabric of liberal democracy. I've since come to see them as its frame. Violence was here. It was present in the racist attacks that were rarely mentioned outside of immigrant families and activist circles. When they were discussed beyond those groups, they were referred to as mere incidents or accidents. A similar thing happened with instances of rape and violence against women which were framed either with stories pertaining to passion ("she pushed him over the edge") or with an attempt to psychologize why some men are just quick to hit or are mean drunks. We would also hear about professors who took advantage of their young students and had a bad reputation. We would hear this said about a student:

"She's fragile. We'll have to pay attention to help her avoid becoming his prey." Everything was happening, and everything was brought up, but it was only within activist circles that the narratives surrounding these events were recognized as structural forms of domination. The narratives explained away those events as violent exceptions, life's pitfalls to be avoided, the result of an individual's psychology, or even Evil with a capital "E." It was the same Evil that was in all of the detective novels, thrillers, and stories about serial killers that were so popular in the 1990s. That was precisely how violence was presented: it was Evil, a monstrous exception that revealed the dark depths of human nature, especially when it came to men.

Then, in the 2000s, it wasn't so much that what had been silenced was slowly being expressed. What changed was the way that we talked about it. Once, we'd imagined a peaceful civil society full of good will, progress, and unity. In this society, acts of violence were uncivilized exceptions or "problems" that needed to be solved. Violence stemmed from an unruly side of human nature that refused to be domesticated. But then we started to tell the story differently, and all forms of violence, power, domination, oppression, and exploitation reappeared as structures governing the social world.

I remember how all of that was set off just as I entered adulthood. It was even clearer to those who were younger than me.

Then everyone picked a side.

After that, the process always proceeds in the same manner: after years of unsuccessfully fighting inequality within a generally peaceful atmosphere, peace becomes identified with powerlessness. So we slam our fists on the table and shout: "We must make our voices heard! Now is the time to act! If we have to throw some bricks through some windows, then that's what we'll do." We start talking about self-defense and an eye for an eye. The definition of violence then begins to gradually change. The definition of legitimate violence also changes incrementally, first with regard to property, then with regard to people. Finally, the conversation surrounding weapons reemerges, among both those for and those against the state, among nationalist and antifa groups, feminists as well as masculinists, etc. And then, here we go again – we have to fight.

At times like that, no one believes in negotiations.

In today's world, peace has worn thin. It's no longer aestheticized. No one – not even the artists who were previously busy creating pretty allegorical doves – is willing to say they want peace without immediately including an addendum. Some people say they only want peace "when there's justice." The opposing camp says it only wants peace "when order is restored." When I was young, many artists and athletes explained themselves cautiously: "I don't want to get into politics. It's divisive, and I would rather try to bring us together." Now, those same people are active participants. They describe themselves as divisive and refer to "our people," "the family," etc. The notion of peace for the sake of peace that was so fetishized in my youth is now like a lifeless puppet. There's no one, or almost no one, left to pull its strings.

And yet, I still believe in this peace, the lie in which I grew up. I still hold on to it, in spite of everything else. I believe in it against the prevailing winds of the times and despite the awareness of power dynamics I now have as an adult. There's at least one reason that keeps me holding on to this: it allows me to think about something other than war, something that isn't a war of all against all. It allows for another *possibility*. It makes it possible to think about desiring something other than what we have and what history has passed down to us. This possibility is beyond class war, culture wars, colonial and postcolonial warfare, domination and how it's envisioned or perceived, power relations, and the bellicose imagination that champs at the bit for a chance to draw its weapons and see truth burst forth in combat.

I therefore believe in irenicism in the face of adversity. This does *not* mean that I think that we're at peace. I don't believe that there's a horizon where we'll find the sort of childish peace that envisions universal reconciliation, where all people and all forms of life exist in harmony. I don't think that we've ever been fighting for that, that it could ever actually be reached, or even that it would be a good idea if we could achieve it.

However, the persistent child within me remains in perpetual debate with both the adolescent that I've been and the adult that I've become. This child's perspective holds onto an idea that, I think, explains everything that I do. I continue to believe that the ongoing widespread war between us is still a *scandal*.

WAR

In a recent work, you wrote about how thinking has a dual role: it both thinks about war and wages it. You also mentioned "an ongoing war between comprehensive thinking that becomes a stranger to itself and defines itself according to its object, and activist thinking that's involved in the conflict, determines the position of the one thinking, and defines itself according to its subject." As you put it, "The first kind of thinking envelops things, while the second attacks and defends." Where do you see daylight between yourself and each of those two positions?

It has taken me a while to understand that there are different sorts of wars going on in all areas of our lives. Even though we might not always take up arms, "war" is still a fitting term for the structure of history.

This wasn't how I thought about things in the beginning. At that time, I didn't understand why some people were so angry. To me, their rage seemed like an irrational outburst. I failed to understand people's hatred, even when that hatred might have seemed justifiable.

I wasn't the least bit interested in competition or in all of the healthy forms of rivalry that the liberal world in which I grew up encouraged. I had no desire to win it all, prove that I was the best athlete, perfect myself through competition, triumph over opponents, or be someone who was "killing the game." All conflict seemed like an anomaly to me. I thought that if we could just talk it out, debate with one another, and come to an understanding of each other's point of view, then we would be able to reconcile even the worst of enemies. When you really got down to it, conflict was nothing more than a mistake, a misunderstanding, a bias, or a temporary blind spot. If we'd just known what was behind this conflict, we wouldn't have been mad at each other.

My entry into adulthood turned this viewpoint upside down, and it was painful. That flipped viewpoint presupposes that we're waging war. That presupposition makes it possible for us to understand human affairs so that we can grasp the state of these beings that are similar and yet different. It seems to me that presupposing peace makes it harder to see things vividly and clearly. By this, I certainly don't mean that this war is necessary, nor is it inscribed in our nature. This is just a historical fact, and a contingent one at that: there are social classes with differing interests. There are different camps. This is just how it happened. There are tribes, clans, the domestication and subjugation of other species, settlements, city-states, slavery, patriarchy, imperialism, colonialism, industrial exploitation, etc. There was no absolute reason for any of it. There's no way to look back at history and retroactively legitimate things. Nevertheless, we can't deny that history either. It's neither a possession nor a truth. Instead, we're its product.

It's simply what's happened, and nothing more. It could have happened otherwise, but it didn't.

All wars and conflicts are the product of history. Broadly speaking, what I call "war" is the absence of something held in *common*. It's an irremediable absence that no negotiation can overcome because our past has been deformed by domination and exploitation. In fact, all possible symmetries between subjects have been broken. Some conflicts run so deep that they determine our very understanding of the terms by which we articulate them, so much so that one side can then deny the conflict's occurrence. This is when we can start calling it a war. At that point, people no longer agree on the facts themselves. There's no agreement about the situation at hand. Some people view things one way, and others view them another way. There's no middle ground where truth can be found. The vision of one group is set against the vision of the other. The victory of one side and triumph of their worldview can only mean the other side's defeat.

Nevertheless, what I retain from my childhood thinking makes me dislike this war. I'll never see this war as a foregone conclusion. There's no reason for that to be the way things are.

That's why I scrupulously avoid any desire for conflict. I don't like confrontation anyway, to such an extent that it's a shortcoming for me in philosophy. I don't like any debate that resembles a duel. I don't like needing to beat someone. If I had to choose, I think I would even prefer to lose. I don't want to convince anyone. I don't share that passion for intellectual conquest cherished by many thinkers who've shifted the desire to vanquish from the field of battle to the symbolic battlefield. I have no desire to captivate, strategize, rhetorically capture an audience, humiliate an opponent and make them submit, or wield arguments and theses like so many weapons until they bend the knee.

I neither like nor want that.

However, as people often mention to me, I always begin by thinking about things in terms of "battle lines" (a term which I've inherited from Althusser), camps, and positions. Why do I do this if I have no desire to engage in war?

I think that it's always good to approach a field involving humanity by projecting the greatest possible degree of warfare onto it. Doing so allows me to begin without assuming that some people are just morons. It lets me avoid thinking that some people are completely in the right and that the others have utterly failed to understand the situation. To the contrary, assuming that there's an ongoing war helps us see that each person has understood who they are, where they are, and what position they defend. This is the first advantage of this approach: it restores everyone's intelligence.

This approach is also advantageous because it conveys the *nervous* nature of the situation. For example, when it comes to aesthetics, my initial interest in a work of art always involves seeing it as a battlefield. I then look for a dispute or something irreconcilable on the battlefield as a sort of pivotal point that allows me to arrange the forces and tensions surrounding it. I could name dozens of examples of this, but here's the first one that comes to mind. When I was a great lover of crime novels, I was particularly interested in the structural differences between "whodunits" – which focus on the use of logic and mind games, like in John Dickinson Carr's locked-room mysteries – and American noir novels – like Mickey Spillane's pulp fiction novels, Dashiell Hammett's early novels, and the works of Raymond Chandler, all of which present the crime novel as a depiction of the social world organized into the categories of police, crime, and corruption. I remember reading Boileau and Narcejac's short book on the crime novel, a perfect little piece of mental machinery that sees noir as a result of the decomposition of detection. At the same time, I was also reading a brief work written by Chandler that gives the noir novel center stage and treats the investigation as little more than a somewhat needless accessory. We can desire to accommodate those two perspectives, but we can't ever wholly reconcile them.

When I understood these aesthetic power dynamics, it felt like I also comprehended the tension that shapes crime literature. In order to explore that tension, I could alternate between taking sides with one group and the other. There were certain moments when investigation fascinated me as a sort of mental askesis. At other times, when I was tired of this formalism, I preferred the noir novel's political morality and its revelatory, cathartic violence.

I want to say that understanding that there's a fundamental conflict within this kind of art also allowed me to recognize what makes up its network of *nerves*. That was also how I became interested in movies, science fiction, television series, etc. I always look for the aesthetic nervous system, the fundamental tension that organizes the field so that it hosts a kind of endless battle.

Generally speaking, whenever we're interested in a specific area, I believe that there's more to be gained intellectually if we presuppose that there's an underlying fundamental and permanent conflict that can't be resolved.

That's how I came to love rock and hip-hop. It's also how I approach anti-speciesism, with welfarism and concern with animals' well-being on one side and abolitionism on the other. There's a similar fundamental conflict in the clash between reform and revolution in the workers' movement.

Everywhere I look, I try to find a center and its margins. I first search for compromises, concessions, and the mainstream. Then, I try to uncover the intractable, the radical, and the underground. This helps as I try to locate the pivotal point of confrontation around which a field of creation, thought, or action revolves. Eventually, this pivotal point is almost always between those who believe in the need to dig in their heels and prepare for confrontation and those who reject that confrontation and prefer moderation. This always makes me think of these lyrics from a Leonard Cohen song: "There is a war between the ones who say there is a war and the ones who say that there isn't."

This war is stronger than Lyotard's "differend" that was often discussed in the 1990s. This kind of war instead structures subjectivities and places them into positions within a field. When I was a student, "discourse ethics" was the dominant paradigm in moral and political philosophy. That paradigm accompanied the very brief and deceptive triumph of liberal democracies in the West. We oscillated between Habermas's conception of the transcendental role of discourse in the constitution of the public sphere and Apel's affirmation that certain principles were always excluded from discourse, including, notably, the possibility of discourse itself. In other words, we can't enter into discussion with those who deny the possibility of discussion. There's an infinite series of possible variations on this question. For example, should the enemies of freedom be free? Should we show tolerance to the intolerant? Here we run into the true contradiction of liberal thinking: if we treat anti-liberals liberally, we allow them to destroy the very possibility of liberty that we claim to support. On the other hand, if we do the opposite, we just prove that, rather than really being liberal, we're actually authoritarians by imposing what we call "liberty" on those who want nothing to do with it. I think that this was the central paradox occupying the life of the mind during the 1990s.

The idea of war is what allowed me to extract myself from this interminable liberal paradox. It's not *discussion* but *war* that structures society. All cultural forms are ongoing wars.

Nevertheless, unlike those who reread Schmitt during those years and rediscovered the virtues of thinking that the truth of politics is war, I detest the idea that war is an existential truth and refuse to believe in the truth of hostility or existential enemies. I think that some people are attracted to the radicality of the bellicose and fascistic texts of Schmitt (*Theory of the Partisan*) and Jünger (*War as an Inner Experience*). These works make war either an ontological structure – for Schmitt, the notion of "hostility" and an existential enemy who allows me to define myself through confrontation – or something natural – as the expression of a primordial bestiality that the progress of civilization restrains. At the end of the day, the idea that they and all of the people who want war are promoting is that war is true *because it is clear*. In war, there are friends and enemies. There will only be one victor in the end, and this is a fight to the death. Pick your side and fight to annihilate the others because there's no longer any hope for compromise. This kind of thinking is seductive. I think that it describes an antagonist waiting deep within us that awakens once the familial memory of conflict and its horrors has gone quiet, after two or three generations have passed in a relative (and deceptive) state of civil peace. However, war is no more true than peace. A sort of general war structures subjectivity, but it's not subjectivity's truth. It's simply a historical fact. There are struggles, and that's how it is. But that struggle is not our truth. As it grows, all we can do is register the fact of its contingency.

This is why there's no reason to want war or to go looking for it. It's also why I distrust anyone who desires it.

I inherited this from my father and my grandfather. The latter was deployed from Algeria to Provence during World War II. From there, he went all the way to Germany. When he was a teenager, my father wrote to the government to claim the medals that my grandfather had never requested. My grandfather hardly ever spoke about the war, what he'd done, or what he'd been made to do. Sometimes, though, he would mention how, when he was young, people in the cafés in Algeria would say that "what we need is a good war." Those were the people who never went off to fight. I often think about his course of action: he fought, but he never liked to fight. He didn't want to do it, and he wouldn't have wanted it for us either.

I think this is the most honorable path that a subjectivity can take. Caught up in a war that's already
underway, we absolutely must think about the confrontation. We can't turn a blind eye to it. We can't just
claim to believe in an illusory peace or a reconciliatory
return to order, which we often hear discussed in the
French Republic. That just masks and accentuates the
conflict. We can't be cowards. We have to occupy our
positions on the field and defend an idea. However, we
must not believe that the battle that we join is the truth
or even necessary. I would also rather not mix into that
combat any authoritarian desire or libidinous and virile
pleasure.

Ever since I was a child, I've heard *virility* equated
with an appetite for war that permeates even the most
minor aspects of existence. Virility is the feeling associated with a living being who only feels alive when they
confront someone else or define themselves in opposition to another being, hoping to gain the upper hand,
subjugate them, and then end or destroy them. This narrative says that women will glorify the most powerful
one, the leader. Women recognize the one who's bold
and assertive in real or symbolic combat. Then, women
join such warriors to procreate and continue the cycle
of life. So, women give life, men raise it in combat, and
then they kill it.

I find this imaginary world based on virility strange. I
never bought into it.

All my life, I've tried to conduct myself and even fight
my battles without embracing a fascistic love of combat.
When I have to fight, well, I will, but I don't attribute
any deep truth to that fight. I don't ontologize it, and
I don't make it the structure of life or the very form of

being. It's nothing more than a fact, and it's unfortunate when it can't be avoided.

Even when I'm among my revolutionary friends who are against authority and for emancipation, my heart aches whenever I sense that bloodlust, the joy some people feel when war appears as an existential truth. When among my own family, I can feel like a stranger if I sense that kind of thirst rising that can change a clash with the police into the desire to physically fight the cops. The same feeling can turn a radical critique of fascism into a desire to joyfully crack some fascist skulls. This is a desire for vengeance: an eye for an eye, a tooth for a tooth, and a life for a life, in the hope of making them pay: "Let them die a fiery death!" Eyes begin to glimmer with excitement when it comes down to a question of "us or them."

I've always run away from this desire for war. Now, as I am today, I try to confront that desire and understand it by looking at it head on from the perspective of as many sides and camps as possible, all without ever sharing that desire.

In all things, my ideal is to think about war without wanting it.

In general, I adopt the viewpoint of a disgruntled universalist. My writing then flows directly from that point of view.

FINDING A VIEWPOINT

Does thinking require us to adopt a viewpoint? Is it instead possible to think without a viewpoint properly speaking, in a way that gives thinking over to its own uncertainty? What kind of viewpoint have you constructed over time and since you began studying philosophy?

Anyone who thinks is always caught up in a war. Their heads start spinning, and, at first, the different camps don't seem to be clear. It's as if the battle lines are constantly in motion. They try to ascertain where they are, but there isn't anywhere to go.

What they lack in such cases is a *viewpoint*. Sometimes we're thrown into the middle of permanent conflicts, opposing views, and facts that different camps interpret in different ways. In order to articulate a thought in those moments, we have to find higher ground, something like a rocky overhang, above the clash of opinions, interests, and discourses. This viewpoint isn't a view from nowhere. It isn't a divine viewpoint that can see from all angles at once. Nor is it a bird's-eye view. It's just a high place, an outcropping that allows us to temporarily escape the situation in order to situate ourselves by seeing – roughly – all of the other positions.

I'm convinced that a theoretical viewpoint is always an abstraction. Therefore, adopting such a view implies extracting, detaching, and removing oneself from a situation, or simulating such a disengagement in thought.

We find Hartsock's theory of a "standpoint" in today's social sciences and in activism that advocates for the recognition of identities. This concept is understood as a "position," an active viewpoint from which a subject is engaged within a field.

However, recognizing one's own viewpoint or position within a social field requires passing through the viewpoint from which one is seen by others. We can only see our own situation if we allow our thinking to let us partially step outside of that situation. So, defining our degree of engagement within a social field requires a degree of disengagement.

My philosophical trajectory and the concomitant progressive construction of my viewpoint are therefore marked by a series of abstractions. I've had to extract myself from my situation and from our situation. When I think about what really counted for me, I think about how the history of my own "standpoint" is bound up with the history of my theoretical influences. I've tried to let my thinking abstract me from my masculinity and to separate the frustrated universality of my viewpoint from the social position of my male body. This has only been possible because I've drawn on my mother's feminism, books from the publishing house Éditions des femmes, Virginia Woolf's *A Room of One's Own*, and texts from materialist feminists like Silvia Federici and Christine Delphy. I'm thinking specifically about texts on the distribution of housework and male strategies for escaping those tasks (e.g. by doing things poorly so that you don't have to do them at all). They've allowed me to have a slightly better understanding of what I'm like from the outside, and they've given me a minimal grasp of the male aspects of my way of being (like devaluing housework while valorizing creation).

My understanding of my class position first came from Marxist texts and later from certain books by Bourdieu. I recognized myself in those privileged students who have the luxury of not needing school and who always pit a deeper knowledge that they've inherited against what they're taught in schools.

In order to see how my viewpoint was white, I needed to read works of colonial history like those by Las Casas and those on the conquest of Mexico. Theory came later, with C. L. R. James and Du Bois first, then Fanon, and now the writings of Tommy Curry and Norman Ajari on Black masculinity. We sometimes talk about being white as an unmarked marker. Toni Morrison has remarked on how difficult it is for white subjects to recognize themselves as white. From her vantage point outside of whiteness, she could see perfectly well what it meant to be white. It was obvious to her. I remember living for a time with the warm and fuzzy impression of being racially neutral. From that viewpoint, I never would have recognized that I'm white.

It didn't take long for me to become aware of my class and gender, but recognizing my whiteness was different. That took a long time.

That understanding required me to recognize not only myself, but also – and especially – my own ignorance about myself and my situation.

Nancy Tuana has written that, like knowledge, ignorance is situated. The changing situation and state of my ignorance regarding my viewpoint as a male, white, and middle-class person have therefore coincided with the history and trajectory of my philosophical education. This process isn't finished. The sometimes violent disengagement of my viewpoint from my being a young, white, middle-class, cisgender, European human being is ongoing. Furthermore, I also try to detach my viewpoint from being human, a living and temporal being. For me, the philosophical construction of a viewpoint goes beyond the bounds of human society. We also have to reconstruct our human viewpoint from the viewpoint of nonhumans, our viewpoint as living beings from the viewpoint of the nonliving, etc.

When I entered the École normale supérieure in the early 2000s and took Dominique Lestel's courses on animal cultures, I became interested in animal ethology and primatology. Then, I discovered animal ethics alongside Jean-Baptiste Jeangène Vilmer and read the *Cahiers antispécistes* [*Antispeciesist Notebooks*] and the works of Florence Burgat. All of this played a part in decentering my viewpoint from the perspective of humanity alone. This informed the perspective from which I wrote the novel *Mémoires de la jungle* [*Memories from the Jungle*], where I tried to take up the point of view of a chimpanzee that's trying to be human.

My perspective on life itself has been most profoundly impacted by the teachings of Quentin Meillassoux,

84

encountering Graham Harman, and reading Ray Brassier (particularly the works that discuss dead matter) and Iain Hamilton Grant (especially "Nature after Nature"). Within this constellation of unique thoughts, which is often referred to as "speculative realism," I've found a project aimed at undoing the correlation between being and thinking. In so doing, it strives to think being without thought and successfully construct a viewpoint on that which has no viewpoint.

Finally, certain things I read as a student allowed me to abstract time and matter, to try to think about "what there is" and the very structures of the possible, and to detach myself from a kind of tyranny of the real. Here, I'm thinking of the Australian school in particular, all reflections on modality, David Lewis's modal realism, Alvin Plantinga's theology, D. M. Armstrong's ontology as well as the thinking of neo-Meinongians like Richard Sylvan and Edward Zalta, and Graham Priest's dialethic logic that moves beyond noncontradiction.

My metaphysical viewpoint was constructed by detaching the possible from a series of things: first from human subjectivity, then from the subjectivity of all living things, and finally from the real.

What is a metaphysical viewpoint?

It's a viewpoint on an idea or a concept that follows from the absence of that idea or concept. Let me explain what I mean by that. What I understand as the metaphysical register of thinking consists of envisioning something from the possibility of its inexistence. This is what metaphysicians do. They abstract from something. This means that they imagine the inexistence of whatever it may be in an attempt to reconstruct it and produce a concept of it. For example, it's only through the possibility of the absence of time that I can try to reconstruct precisely what I understand "time" to be. I would otherwise be unable to distinguish "time" from everything else, and I would conflate everything with time. The same thing goes for humanity. If I'm unable to think through the possibility of humanity's inexistence, whether from before its appearance or after its disappearance, then my thinking would be confined and limited. Humanity would become transcendental and a condition of possibility for everything else. In this way, speaking about the world would actually just mean speaking about the human world. At the same time, anything that I say about humanity would also apply to the world.

Abstraction is therefore the fundamental operation of metaphysical thinking. This abstraction entails constructing the possibility of the inexistence of that about which one is trying to think. It's the higher ground, the rocky overhang that we've been trying to find. It's a thing's possible inexistence. Contemplating a thing makes us think from *the possibility that it might not be*. To make a thing appear in thought, I have to remove it and then reconstitute it as an idea.

To philosophize is to construct a viewpoint. This requires doing two things at once: concretely situating oneself within the social field and detaching and disengaging one's thought so it can reach abstraction. The history of a philosophy's creation is always the history of a viewpoint's creation. We see this with the Cartesian subject, the empirical subject, the Kantian transcendental ego, the Husserlian intentional consciousness, etc.

What would be the fundamental definition of your philosophical viewpoint?

In theoretical thought, I hope to establish a continuity between two projects: the project of situating the viewpoint of subjectivity and its position – which has more to do with the social sciences and politics – and the project of theoretically elaborating a viewpoint from the absence of a viewpoint – which is a metaphysical matter. My hope is to be able to think of myself and all of us through not only the historically constructed things that determine us like our class, race, and gender, but also through determining factors like species, life, materiality, and temporality. I hope to simultaneously think of myself and us in these ways *from the viewpoint of the possible.*

SOLITUDE

*Your viewpoint is somewhat on the margins of the domi-
nant positions in thinking. Do you ever feel a certain
sense of solitude due to the way that you construct this
viewpoint?*

My disengaged viewpoint certainly isolates me.
Currently, I don't really fit in with any movements or
schools. Sometimes, that's a weakness.

This point of view emerges out of a complicated and
definitely still unfinished process of construction. When
working with social and political concepts, the way that
this viewpoint abstractly disengages from our situation
is too much like metaphysics. At the same time, when
thinking metaphysically, this point of view is too close
to social and political concepts.

As of right now, some of my works have benefitted
from a positive misunderstanding, and others have
benefitted from a negative misunderstanding. For example, the reception of *Form and Object* shows what I
mean by a positive misunderstanding. It was labeled

as a work of "speculative realism," even though I knew nothing about that burgeoning movement while I was writing it – and despite the fact that I was taking Quentin Meillassoux's courses. Furthermore, that work had hardly anything at all to do with New Realism, an ephemeral fad with which that work is nevertheless still associated. *The Life Intense* has been read and liked, but often from strange angles that I never would have expected. Some have seen it as praising intensity. Others think that it radically critiques intensity and instead advocates for reducing the speed of existence as ideal. I always thought of it as more of an example of a metaphysical test anchored in an analysis of our situation. It tested an idea from within our concrete condition in the here and now. How and why did that idea appear? What purpose does it serve? I wanted to find that idea's breaking point and see how we might protect it from itself by avoiding making it absolute. I wanted to consider the unexamined, un-deconstructed value of the deconstruction of all values and all oppositions. I wanted to map a genealogy of pure variation, of intensity, that is, a norm that denounces all norms. But the work hasn't really been received that way.

Even if some people find what I do intriguing, I'm still not sure that I've been understood.

Some philosophers today defend a specific way of life, like being queer. They certainly seem to be more immediately effective. Paul Preciado does this very well. There are also other ways of thinking that propose models of being that are keyed to or prioritize living things like animals or plants. There are metaphorical theories positing new values that point toward what's supposed to be good, like intensity, transition, metamorphosis, or mixture. They present these good values against their bad counterparts from the past, like identity, eternity, or substance. This calls to mind some of Bruno Latour's followers and Emanuele Coccia's works. More broadly, there's an understandable call for philosophies to draw sharp contrasts, propose a way of life, or provide us with a model for what we *must* be and think from here on out. However, what interests me is what we still *can* be and think in our current conditions. We want philosophies with consequences. We want to be able to derive a philosophy's moral and political effects right here and right now, in this very moment. By contrast, I find that a more fitting metaphysics is one that lets us think about all possible lives and all possible acts. Who needs philosophy in order to act? Saying that you do sounds more like an excuse: "Look, the reason why I did this and why I acted like that is because there's this book where they explain that that's what you're supposed to do." I have no desire to provide people with excuses. I don't want to tell anyone how they should live. The worst thing would be for someone to draw any sort of "you must" from my thinking. I want no imperatives in my thinking. We have our whole lives for what we *must* do. When I think, I would like once more to find what we *can* do.

As a result, my point of view and my way of doing things are a little isolated today. I have no complaints about that. It's very understandable that this is the case, for multiple reasons. First, the work that I'm trying to construct is still underway and will take time. I'm not entirely satisfied with what I've done up to this point. Second, my project really isn't about illuminating what's happening in the present, but rather reflecting on what comes next and opening a space for possibility.

My thinking would be useless if it was solely to arm us in the here and now, within the scope of actual struggles for things that should make our lives better, like decolonization, emancipation, equality, freedom from oppression, alliances with other species, lasting global sustainability, etc. Others have already engaged in thinking that supports these goals. Those thoughts continue life and actions with words. We engage in activism and push for compliance with our aims. But what interests me and what I know how to do instead involves anticipating the possible effects of the authority that's supposed to free us from all authority or the possible normative effects of the deconstruction of norms. In other words, I'm interested in how the very things that offer possibilities can have effects that do the opposite. My goal is to find ways of thinking that preserve possibility and never take a "you can" and petrify it into a "you must be able to."

At its core, my ideal is simple: I think in the hope of building a communal space for thinking that will be available for those who come after. In the coming years, I would like to do my best to prepare this place so that those who might one day need this viewpoint might find it already explored, well constructed, and ready to serve their purposes. I want to prepare a space for the possible with a sound architectural base.

What I'm trying to construct is a habitable model of subjectivity, of a way of being and of a way of thinking. I'm trying to do this while being faithful to the possible in a way that lets beings be, so that they can be distinguished without undergoing hierarchization and differentiated without losing their equality. I also try to avoid both imposing the values of life on thought and forcing the values of thought on life.

As I move through different domains, I'm always trying to clear up the facts, sketch out the battle lines, map the conflicts, and uncover something that may still seem unusual and strange, but that may be a commonplace communal space in the future.

Thinking has to do some reconnaissance in order to construct this future communal place. This doesn't imply resurrecting the myth of the avant-garde. Instead, it's just a thought's somewhat solitary scouting mission in search of a path of ideas within the undergrowth of the present and the past. Perhaps that thought will lose its way or be forgotten. And yet, it might lead to a place worth looking into and preparing as best it can for others that might come along. I hope that others will find it one day, move in, and rebuild their nest and world there.

ACTIVISTS

Alongside your philosophical work, or even at its heart, you show an interest in a life of activism and the political space. How do you understand activist thinking as opposed to a more conceptual or metaphysical thinking?

I don't think I can respond abstractly to that question. My relationship with activism has always been a relationship with activists, which is to say, with actual beings. I'm not talking about the intolerable bad faith activists, or those who are just riding the wave of the current moment and only become activists when necessary to serve their opportunism. I'm referring to sincere activists whose engagement brings them nothing but the occasional personal satisfaction and sense of camaraderie, along with a lot of problems and sometimes even hatred.

The first person I think of is Denis, one of my two fathers. He was still involved in activism when I was a child and during my adolescence, when our home had the politically charged atmosphere in which I was formed. He came from Trotskyism, to which he remained faithful, from the Revolutionary Communist League to the New Anticapitalist Party. He was especially engaged in anti-racist politics. When I think of him, I remember how all of his movements and positions seemed to actually communicate this: "I'm doing what I think is best, but I don't know that it's good." He never had the kind of attitude that some activists exhibit that makes those who are not involved out to be guilty: "And what about you? What are you doing for the cause?" He did what he did without asking anyone else to do the same. He believed in what he did, but he believed in it for himself, and he also had his doubts. He had a sense of humor and a certain distance with regard to his involvement with the League that contrasted with the seriousness of the "soldier-monks." He was always able to be self-deprecatory while also being extremely generous with his time and energy by protesting, attending joint meetings, distributing leaflets, etc. He came from a Catholic educational background, and he eventually suspected that his engagement had religious roots because he knew that his activism was first and foremost a moral conviction, a faith of sorts, and never a fact, an obligation, or a necessity.

He was a Marxist and a philosophical materialist, but he also distrusted secular, atheist materialism and remained sympathetic to religious engagement. I think that his impression that political radicality was accompanied by a fascination with violence gnawed at him for a long time. At a certain point, a revolution involves killing people or it's just idle intellectual talk. Perhaps he felt that violent impulse within himself before it disgusted him. Now, when he recognizes it in a comrade or within the ranks of his own organization or camp, it repulses him just as much as the enemy's fascism.

I think that he's always sought the path of the just and taken the side of the humble, knowing full well that history, which is as unfathomable as God's ways, might eventually prove him wrong. We wouldn't really know until some day, later, perhaps long after death.

As an adolescent, I joined many comrades. Some of them later moved into alter-globalization, and others participated in the initial stages of something that we called "*appelisme*" (autonomism), as though we were speaking our own secret language. That name was a reference to *Appel*, a short text that young autonomists saw as a faithful guide. The same can be said for *The Coming Insurrection*, which was put out by veteran members of *Tiqqun*. The "*appelistes*" were determined to abandon the life that they were expected to lead and work instead toward an immediate insurrection. This meant breaking with aging organizations of communists, leftists, and the worker's movement. They wanted to put an end to the same old syndicalist processions of activists who've become too civilized and had compartmentalized their domesticated, bourgeois lives from their engagement in the struggle. After a personal crisis, one follower of "*appelisme*" dropped out of school and even stopped playing music to set off to find comrades and another way of living. He chose the kind of frontline, avant-gardist violence of those who lead modern autonomous demonstrations and sabotage the capitalist administration of the world. We had long discussions about all of this as we walked along the canal at night. Those discussions reminded me of Jack London's *White Fang* and *The Call of the Wild*. There we were, a wild dog who wanted to be domesticated and a pet dog who wanted to run wild and live in the woods. He might have occasionally envied my life. Ever since I'd settled in – albeit precariously – first as a student and then as a civil servant teacher, I had time to write and theorize. I was becoming a professional intellectual. As for me, I also somewhat envied his ability to break away and his radical praxis, even though he struggled to write a bit here and there as he moved from one active crisis to another. Surrounded by battle-hardened comrades, he felt that writing didn't really do much and theory was a luxury.

This is an old story of an intellectual who feels guilty in the presence of a professional activist. Luckily, our friendship prevented us from sliding down the slippery slope of mutual jealousy and frustration. Even though I'm not sure where he currently stands on this, I still admire now what I admired then: the intransigence that let him see years in advance what was bound to collapse and would not remain. Because I wanted to be respectful of the present situation and certain of its social rules, laws, and ways of doing things, I sometimes felt like he would go too far. Every time I felt that way, he was just doing something that would be considered normal by those around me a few years later. These were things like breaking windows but not attacking people, looting but with the aim of redistribution, and materially attacking the system that I was content to critique in the abstract. Nevertheless, during our discussions, he also needed the words and concepts that we shared even though we didn't completely agree with one another. He needed something of the abstract possibility without which action, lacking a horizon, becomes meaningless and directionless.

I hope he's doing well.

When I published my first novel, *Hate: A Romance*, he teased me a little because I was fully entering the establishment, even though I was still stalled on its threshold, caught between rebellion and conformism. At that time, I met Jean Le Bitoux, a gay rights activist with historical importance to the movement. He'd read my manuscript. While he put forward some critiques, he still thought that it was good and recognized in it a moment in history that I hadn't witnessed. He invited me and my partner out several times and talked about the comrades he'd lost, the days he'd spent at the Père-Lachaise Cemetery, and how AIDS had been like a war. He lived on his memories. He was elegant and worldly, but also somewhat otherworldly and out of sync with most people at that time. He died a few months later.

In that book, there's a character who shares many of the same traits with Didier Lestrade. Lestrade is a central figure for ACT UP Paris and a great music critic and house music promoter in France. Like Larry Kramer in the US, he's an activist who changed what it means to be an activist, situated somewhere between the Communist Party and the emergence of social networks. He really is the missing link in French activism. He was very angry with me. I was too young when I wrote the novel, and I would never write it that way if I could do it again today. I greatly admire Lestrade from afar. He's clearly complex. He's a model for the kind of unapologetic activist driven by their rage and anger. Activists like that reserve their affections for those who are close to them. They expose their bodies and their persons, without fear of insults. They detest postponements, concessions, and political careerism. Their words match their actions.

I think that they also feel bitter about not having been recognized like they should have. Lestrade's struggle began for gay rights, and then it grew to include other minority groups. That struggle was intersectional before the term was popular. He was one of the first people to sound the alarm that his struggle's heritage was being redirected. He warned that part of the gay population was moving to the right and into "homonationalism," a tool that the far right and populists use against Muslims by making the defense of gay rights seem like proof of Western civilization's opposition to the barbarism of the colonized.

Along with a few other people, Lestrade introduced a way of personalizing activism in France. He invented a way for people to inextricably link their persons, desires, angers, and hatreds to the ideas that they defend by giving their bodies to the cause.

I published my first novel at the same time that another book appeared by my then-future friend, Jean-Baptiste Del Amo. He was becoming increasingly engaged in the struggle for animal rights and began his ongoing activism with the organization L214. Our discussions and a trip we took to a livestock farm in the Vendée played a role in his awareness of and engagement in that struggle. As for me, I became a vegetarian and began to follow the anti-speciesist movement. I wrote about this, but without taking sides in the same way that allowed him to bring his acts and ideas into alignment. He decided to become consistent and fight against the system that exploits nonhuman animals. Since then, I've met many students who've made the same choice, and it's not just about what they eat. Almost everything that they do is governed by the need to be consistent with the idea of a just coexistence with other beings that live, feel, and suffer. They uphold this justice, and they're right when they say that the industrial exploitation of animals is untenable. Overcoming it means rethinking society and developing a politics for all living beings. Sue Donaldson and Will Kymlicka's *Zoopolis* had a strong impact on my understanding of that situation, but it's a politics of the future, something close to science fiction. The real challenge emerges each time that we have to return to the here and now, where the cause of the future is mixed together with complex social considerations. How can we avoid humiliating the butchers and ranchers who think that they're just doing their jobs, and doing them well? How can we be convincing without lecturing, reprimanding, or preaching? It's a calling for some activists. All of the activists of that kind that I know don't fit with how they're often caricatured. Instead, they doubt, tremble, and waver. They think that what they defend is right, but they aren't sure that they're defending it in the right way.

Those misgivings make an activist strong in the face of adversity.

I belatedly crossed paths with activists from the Parti des indigènes de la République (PIR, Party of the Indigenous Peoples of the Republic), whose texts I'd long been reading. I've always been stunned by the ostracism that Houria Bouteldja faced. It was probably due to her having been the first leader of that movement in France. Even though I disagree with some of what she has to say, I often think her interventions are right. They have an Algerian sense of humor about them that reminds me a little of my *pied-noir* family members who grew up there. It involves a sort of mockery mixed with mischief, and it can also be a political weapon. Whenever she's being ironic, they make her pay for it: "Look at what she wrote word for word! She's homophobic and anti-Semitic!" When she is sincere, people instead accuse her of double talk: "It seems like she's condemning the attacks, but that's just so she can actually . . ." I've encountered her on a couple of occasions, and she is the way that she writes. Indigenism is gaining ground right now, but she hardly gets any credit for that. However, she also provides a model for activists. This reminds me of a very beautiful text by Louisa Yousfi, who is close with Houria Bouteldja. It describes the dread that she felt when she had to present a controversial text to a packed room. I think that what she said is both justified and ahead of the current state of studies on indigenous masculinity and the treatment of racialized men. With her permission, I'm here reproducing that text:

I gave this presentation two years ago at the Bandung du Nord. I alluded to the question of non-white men while drawing heavily on the work that had been patiently developed by members of the PIR who had come before me, and especially that of Houria Bouteldja, who had been shouted down and dragged through the mud for that very work. At that time, she was called an "accomplice for the pigs," a "misogynist," an "antifeminist of the first degree," a "reactionary," a "gender traitor," a "bad sister," etc.

I remember enduring having some mud slung at me for similar reasons. Because I wasn't anywhere near as courageous as Houria, I fought with my organization to delay publishing that presentation. When it was published, I crossed my fingers and hoped that it would be read by as few people as possible and prayed that people would leave me alone. Some of my friends even teased me for that, saying that I better watch out. In the end, I received many compliments – all of them in private – and some insults – all of them in public. It was nothing compared to the organized cowardly slander that has been Houria's daily lot in life for more than fifteen years. What can I say? That's the privilege handed down to me.

Today, thanks to the great strides that have been made in the struggle against police violence targeting non-white men, I see blossoming all around me what are essentially the same ideas that we defended in front of that audience as they dreamed of watching us stumble, fall, and never get up again. As humans, we were trembling, but as activists, we held our heads high.

I'm not an activist myself, but this is the best image that I've ever seen of activism. That's precisely what I see in the people whom I admire for their engagement. As Louisa Yousfi says, as humans, they tremble, but they hold their heads high.

NUANCED MINDS AND
ROUGH MINDS

For you, what place does nuance hold in the act of thinking? What is its function? Is it necessary, or can we do without it as soon as we come up with a working theory?

Nuance! Let's appeal to Camus: "We are fighting over nuances, but these nuances are as important as humanity itself." Today, we think it's wrong to make radical judgments and be rigid when we should instead always be able to compromise. This is because nothing is seen as absolute. Nothing is ever absolutely black or white.

This calls to mind the notion of "complexity" that was upheld when Edgar Morin was highly influential. It's the same thing that happens ad infinitum when doubt is given supreme value within simplistic forms of skepticism. In such moments, complexity becomes an overly simplistic concept, and doubt becomes a profession of faith. There's always a point at which the endless call for nuance deprives thinking of its nuance and makes it seem rough.

Rough minds make judgments based on *camps*, while nuanced minds make judgments based on *fields*. Rough minds make decisive conclusions. They're the kind of people who broadly assess ecology as the "new opium of the masses" and "autonomists" as the young petite bourgeoisie in revolt. They see "reactionaries" or "the bourgeoisie" as really just a bunch of despicable bastards who are so dangerous that we should band together to fight them. Their thinking stakes out the position of one camp and its opposition. And that's all there is to it. For them, things are just that simple. It doesn't take long to identify a rough mind and the limits of their thinking. At least rough minds aren't deceitful. They're candid about what they think.

Nuanced minds are more delicate. They do not immediately choose which camp is theirs. A nuanced thinker begins with an assessment that "it's more complicated than that." They pay careful attention to the divisions that emerge between the different factions within each camp. This allows them to see tensions that would otherwise escape notice. They detect underlying conflicts and a whole wealth of complex characteristics. Their judgment is thereby based on *fields*. For example, a nuanced mind that studies far right families is obliged to distinguish between thousands of different kinds of ideals, values, and strategies. There are Traditionalist Catholics, Neopagans, Identitarians, Patriots, those who are Republicans and those who are not, conservatives, reactionaries, electoralists, activists, etc. A nuanced thinker uncovers a field of forces where a rough thinker only sees a block or a monolithic camp.

However, by declaring that the very purpose of thinking lies in being ever more exact, constantly further differentiating between everything that we identify, and refusing to trust broad categories in any domain, a nuanced mind only postpones the moment when they have to draw a battle line and fix a camp, giving a field its substance and consistency. Nuanced minds stall. They detect the cracks of the real within the broad categories employed in the reasoning of others. Those cracks always then reveal increasingly fine distinctions. This leads nuanced minds to hedge and equivocate. They put off the decision that one rightfully expects to follow from their assessment. They delay establishing camps and their position. This is because nuanced minds also have an enemy: rough minds. When it comes to them, nuanced minds are also rigid and prone to idealization. When interacting with rough minds, nuanced minds lump things together into a block, and have a camp – even if they don't want to admit it.

I think that when overly nuanced minds examine objects in order to make a judgment, everything becomes a question of scale and minute details. I know this tendency because I feel it in myself. Even smaller-scale, more refined generalizations are still generalizations. They too should be further clarified. The process is never-ending. We should recognize refined differences between subgenres. For example, we can never just say that we love or hate the entirety of hip-hop. *It's more complicated than that.* By paying equal attention to the different varieties and nuances, such painstakingly scrupulous judges infinitely postpone the moment when camps are determined and positions declared. They sharpen the idea of difference as much as possible. However, by never stopping their thinking, nuanced minds become entangled by the very concept that organizes their thinking. The concept of a "field" lets nuanced minds infinitely divide any domain of culture. This mires their thinking in minuscule details, which makes nuanced minds lose sight of the bigger picture. They forget about the very thing that gave substance to the object under examination. Their unsubstantial reasoning evaporates into a cloud of subtle details.

All they do is push back the moment of roughness, the moment when we have to draw the line. That moment arrives for every kind of thinking, and there's no avoiding it. If that moment never comes, our judgment slips through our fingers like sand and dissolves into the deceptive appearances of real continuities. These can make it seem as if there never were any opposition or contradiction between us. Too much finesse makes us miss what's most obvious. We lose sight of the conflicts and battle lines on the horizon. A rough mind might be astigmatic, but a mind with too much nuance ends up being severely shortsighted.

That's why I don't trust the fetishization of nuanced thinking.

RADICALNESS

As opposed to the ambiguous art of nuance, do you think that a radical posture is better suited for the exercise of thinking?

I'm convinced that everything that's true about us is born out of radicalness. I also think that that's where it dies.

This is not a very well-supported theory. It's more like an intuition that guides me. Whether in art, music, literature, or politics, I've always searched for the truth being told in a way that the dominant culture hasn't yet acknowledged. I look to the margins, where nascent ideas are accused of excess and violence.

I myself don't always produce radical work because I try to understand everything and to include contrary and opposing positions. That's my contradiction. But I'm drawn to radicalness. Sometimes I even express a rather unfair disdain for works or ideas that don't originate from a desire for a radical break with the dominant culture.

There are, of course, "centrist" works and ideas that have a part to play and a charm of their own. Some things that have been popularized are also excellent. I don't think that accommodation immediately equals corruption or that it's always bad to aim for a broad audience and try to please everyone. But that doesn't stimulate my mind. I don't think that anything truthful arises from that. Instead, it just rewrites things, rearranges them a little more clearly, and makes them mainstream. I'm never inspired to think by anything that's middling, moderate, or a product of negotiation.

Nevertheless, it might well be said that my thinking always negotiates between radically opposed points. This is because I think there's a difference between being true and being right. We can be true in a moment or a situation and still do something false or be wrong with that truth. A truth in no way indicates that those who bring it forth are right. They can still be totally wrong.

The truth of a situation can often be violent. It's born out of a situation in which some individuals no longer wish to compromise with the values of others. It's also very often accompanied by a desire to free oneself from any constraints that might relativize the idea. That kind of truth wants to break free from life – and it's willing to kill if necessary. This is a terroristic truth.

There's something paradoxical about those who defend that kind of radical, almost *mortal*, truth. The paradox lies in the fact that they're wrong, but they make us see something true about us, them, or the situation. However, they arrive at a poor compromise between that truth and life. They turn it into death.

In cases like this, something true about our condition, us, or them is born out of that radicalness, but that's also where it dies. This is because to be radical is to refuse to compromise. It means disregarding all other demands. A radical truth is no longer encumbered by the need to coexist with *other truths*.

A radical truth claims that it's the only one. Its lack of community is what makes it stand out. However, its radicalness also makes it eclipse and stifle other truths. A radical truth is the opposite of a community of truths. Radical truths frequently die from their exclusive, sovereign solitude. They refuse to intermingle or compromise. Their initial brilliance becomes blinding, and their initial singularity becomes restrictive.

If we want to bring a truth to life, we have to introduce it into society and present it to its peers by introducing it to other truths and other urgent, pressing values – like not killing people. We might say that truth can be civilized. It can become accustomed to being around others so that it can learn to negotiate and be negotiated.

Seen from a radical viewpoint, this is the story of the domestication of a truth that was once naked, pure, and untamed. This is the story of its socialization, and also of its betrayal. It's true that it will fade and lose some of its former brilliance. It becomes less distinct and more adulterated. One day, it will be completely worn out. Then where will we find a new truth to light the way?

That's when it's time to turn to the radical again, because that's where truth is born.

My own position in this regard is tenuous and sometimes frightening, even to me. I think that people who are looking for direction and searching for a true or just idea to orient their journey have to take the risk of plunging into radicalness to try to find there a nascent idea. If they stay too long within the blazing realm of radicalness, they risk being blinded. That's why they have to pluck that idea from its radical cradle, so to speak, feed it, help it grow, and raise it. They have to socialize it among other half-truths, knowing all the while that doing so will make it lose its initial raw force.

This is where truth survives, surrounded by a community of negotiated truths where a reasonable being can try to respond to multiple demands at once. Admittedly, being in that community weakens the truth a bit too. But that's just the way it is.

THE ENEMY

How would you define the category of "enemy" within the field of thinking? What would that enemy look like?

An enemy is an adversary that we hate. Hate plus adversaries equals hostility. I've long thought that it would be better to die than have an enemy. I don't want any hostility. I wouldn't know how to live with it.

Having an enemy is both dazzling and blinding. It's a feeling that galvanizes us without fail. It allows us to direct our force and our energy toward an adverse idea that has been incorporated and incarnated into one or more living bodies. This is how we can despise fellow humans and vow to destroy them. A combination of psychological, moral, and political considerations is mixed into the enemy figure. The enemy is a particularized generality. It's a concretized abstraction. Its concreteness comes from what we personally hate, the features of our fellow humans that physically disgust us. This may be caused by things like the attitudes of others, the looks on their faces, their satisfaction, their cynicism, their bad faith, etc. Could it be that we envy them? Or do we pity them for having to lead this existence? Whatever the case may be, we hope that they'll be destroyed. The list of potential enemies is endless: there's that guy I met whose presence felt like a subjugation to which I sometimes had to submit; that little dictator whose orders I was forced to obey while suffering my humiliation in silence; that horrible husband; that revolting kid; that classmate that got everything they wanted without the slightest effort; that shamelessly capricious brat; that uncle who always yelled racist jokes during family dinners; that same uncle who now complains about how he isn't allowed to say anything anymore; that unbearable coworker; that jackass politician that I see on television year after year who always gets away with everything. We're talking about all of the beings that I hate, the ones that I identify in my imagination as fakes and phonies. I know very well that they lie with impunity, that they got everything that I have without putting in the same effort as me, or that they already have something that I'll never have. That's how the enemy is incarnated, but that alone isn't enough. Hostility always requires something more than just hatred. It also needs a generalization, an abstraction, or an idea. Then, as if by magic, the idea that I oppose takes on a body that descends into my hatred, and, like a Greek god taking on its mortal form, it has a face from then on. And there it is: *that's the enemy*. It's a bastard formed from an idea that I oppose and my own personal hatred. My disgust then starts to feed my arguments against that idea, and vice versa. Once this virtuous – or, perhaps, vicious – circle of animosity is set into motion, everything within a person who embodies the ideas that I fight confirms my opposition. Whenever I see how they act, live, and, in fact, concretely are, I feel a repulsion that feeds my opposition to the idea. Then, as if by a miracle, all of the people that I dislike fall into the category of people who champion the very ideas that I fight.

In this way, a person's peculiar grin or way of moving their mouth becomes indistinguishable from their errors and faults. My rejection of communism is conflated with my disgust for a certain unionist, including their clothes, their hairstyle, the music that they listen to, their awkward sense of humor, etc.

The enemy is a monster. It's a personified stereotype.

The enemy justifies my intellectualized vulgarities. It forces me to bring shits, scumbags, and bastards into the realm of ideas. It's the "leftist sheep" or the "fascist pig." It's calling the people "filthy masses" and calling the government the "rat bastards." For the media, it's either the "shills" or those who spread "fake news." In right-wing parlance, it's the "Islamo-leftists." It used to be the "Judeo-Bolsheviks." It's the "deplorables" and "the rabble."

I don't know if having an enemy is ever a strength. Maybe it could be, but not for me. Perhaps it makes it possible to act or clarifies the meaning of an action. It undoubtedly paints a bull's-eye on a person by mixing them with an idea. As Huysmans wrote, we never really attack the idea without destroying the person. But that isn't how my worldview operates.

I refuse to believe that humanity can only act, desire, and struggle when it has enemies.

That's why I try to dissociate the things that I hate from the adversaries that I face. I don't have to force this because it's just part of my temperament. I do hate certain things, and I think that's healthy. I just try to see those things for what they really are: the expression of my personal likes and dislikes. They're personal judgments that have to do with my situation and how I see, hear, and feel things. I hate, but I never turn it into a matter of ideas.

Whenever I'm confronted by adversaries, I try as much as possible not to hate. I work against them, I face them, and I fight them, but there's no reason for me to hate someone who opposes me.

Is it really possible to confront adversaries without psychologizing them? I don't know. I would imagine that doing so brings a certain *chivalry* to the battle. I might be mistaken because my cultural background offers me limited experience with this. But, it seems to me that the majority of human cultures have some sort of equivalent to chivalric virtues, be they masculine or feminine. I think that this is the case even though the development of increasingly authoritarian civilizations and empires led to a male monopolization of chivalry. Nevertheless, it's still a code for honorable conduct, a set of rules governing behavior. It seems to me that what all of these codes share in common is their goal of teaching the chivalric subject how to be adversarial without being hateful. I very much love the different versions of this that we can see in Bushido, chivalric virtues, and the Amazons' codes of honor, all of which teach us how to fight well.

I have my own little mental theater where I watch friends and adversaries contend with each other. I maintain a silent discussion with them as I write. I feel like I'm psychically responding to one or another of them. It's like I'm jousting with them as I reformulate my argument. I'll try to turn a still very fragile idea around so that I can protect it from the attacks that I anticipate from a certain way of thinking. I'm like a little knight who puts hatred aside. Against the opposition, I try to defend my thinking, which I enrich through different arguments and bouts.

What I hate is my concern alone.

FRIENDS

On the other hand, what's your understanding of a friend,
whether in thinking or in life itself?

What does it mean to be friends? Being friends brings
war to a halt. It's peace, but a lively kind of peace.

Just like anyone else, I need the promise of this kind
of steady peace in life.

I'm an only child, and my first intellectual mentors
were my parents. The education that they gave me made
me happy and curious. This made them my first com-
panions in thought, and they remain that to this day.

For the last twenty years, I've also been in love with
the same person. We're lovers, and we're also friends.
We talk all the time. Even though people sometimes say
we sound the same on the phone, we've never been completely alike. In fact, we're very different. I would have
no way of knowing how much of what I think and write
comes from Agnès. I'm also not sure that she would be
able to say exactly how much of what she does comes
from me. Nevertheless, each of us is clearly the author of

our own work. We aren't two halves of a whole. It isn't a fusion, because if it was, then our love and friendship would be lost within a larger and slightly narcissistic me.

Throughout our lives, we've sought after a love that is equal. Between her job and her work and my job and my work, we've always made absolutely sure that no one has had to sacrifice anything for the other. We let each other be as much as possible, but we also support each other and make each other stronger. It can be hard, and we've had to fumble our way through while still loving each other. Sometimes, we're like two beings searching for balance who, leaning this way and that, almost make each other fall, but then we catch each other and pull each other upright again.

Despite being so close to her, I've still never been able to determine the source of Agnès's joy and force. In conversations, she's comfortable not only speaking but also encouraging others to speak. She abhors it if anyone is excluded or forgotten. She learns things quickly and well. Even when she's thinking abstractly, her mind overflows with empathy and sensitivity. She can therefore always quickly understand the thoughts of others because she's willing to take their principles on board. She gives every thought a chance to see if it works or not, even when it repels her, she doesn't share any of its values, or she finds its effects unacceptable. She doesn't like things that are false or contrived, things that try to pass themselves off as authentic, or anything ordinary that claims to be unique. She detests posturing and anything that tries to put on airs. Those are her values. However, she's ready to hear and try to understand how those things she detests might be defended or how their meaning might be seen in a different light. She sees, hears, and feels thought everywhere. She's no snob. She lightens serious situations, but she also takes things that may seem light very seriously.

Having begun with Aristotle, her research then turned to the Frankfurt School, Adorno, and critical theory, and at the same time to music. She loved Adorno's demanding model of subjectivity, a form of dialectical thinking and critique that's never resolved. She sometimes recognizes something of that thinking in what I do, which I resist, because I feel less critical than that. She knows what I mean, and she pushes me to make my reasoning a little clearer. She has less of a taste for metaphysics and abstraction than I do, but I think that she sees in it a mental game that might serve as an example, a discipline, or a model for how to think in other domains like culture, aesthetics, or other living forms of expression.

She has always accepted the premise of what I'm trying to think. She takes it seriously, with an air of concentration, like someone who plays by the rules. She helps me understand whether or not it works. Nothing that thinks is alien to her, but she also knows how to break away from thinking. When I was an adolescent tumbling through the abyss of fetishized reflexivity and a sort of formalism, she taught me how to come out of it. One day, I told her I was afraid of eventually becoming trapped in my own system. She's always showed me how to find a way out.

Everything that I think comes from me, but it also passes through her.

I think that this is the case for us both.

I also have other close friends who've read my writing when almost no one else was interested in it, and they treated it like it mattered. Talking with these friends, Perrine Bailleux and Flora Katz, allowed me to develop my way of thinking. I tried to construct my own viewpoint through their viewpoints. A few years ago, they also helped me understand that what I was writing risked seeming ineffective at first glance, as if it lacked power and decisiveness. They help me sharpen my thinking. By putting up an amicable resistance, these friends taught me to ensure that my thinking would have an impact. That's the best thing that can happen while constructing a system of thought.

I'm terrible at debating. In an intellectual conflict, I completely shut off. However, friends like those give me the confidence that I need to try out a budding idea that has never seen the light of day beyond my thinking and writing. Those friends' minds are the daylight where these burgeoning ideas either wilt or blossom. They ask questions that aren't an a priori attack on the motives behind my thinking, and they take my endeavors seriously. In this way, they encourage my thinking by helping me see what parts of it don't work without destroying the whole thing. They also introduce me to other fields of thought.

After completing my studies, other friends came along, like Mathieu Bonzom, Arnaud Despax, Ivan Trabuc, Martin Dumont, Laurent Dubreuil, Martin Fortier (who has since died), Donatien Grau, Laurent de Sutter, Léonard Haddad, Vincent Normand, Charles Sarraute, and many others I'm forgetting. There have been many theoretical discussions in cafés, on mountain hikes, and whenever life brings us back together.

In most cases, these friendships were one-on-one. However, there was at least one time when I had the opportunity to experience a larger-scale collective friendship, in a communal space in northern France that was established by the choreographer and theoretician Jan Ritsema. I was invited there to give a presentation in English on theses from *Form and Object*.

I wasn't sure what to do. I didn't really understand why I'd been invited, and I was afraid I might be speaking to a cult. That had already happened to me once, when I was invited to a "speculative" gathering in a beautiful Parisian apartment by a group of people who were clearly searching for a new guru to replace the one who'd just died. But this time was different. It was a group of curious young people from all different countries. That discussion with them is still ongoing.

My English isn't very good, and I struggled at first. It was hard work. But then, I became excited once the first questions were thrown my way, interrupting my presentation. For the first time, I was able to collectively discuss that book's theses with doctoral students, artists, and activists too, all of whom were sitting or lying on blankets. They all took my presuppositions seriously. They accepted the initial stipulations, played along with me, and understood the motivation behind this abstract game. There weren't enough seats for everyone in the "peacock room" where I was speaking, at the end of the building's right wing, so some people watched the debate on screens in other rooms.

I can remember my feelings of exhilaration, freedom, and accomplishment. That thought wasn't just confined to me. It could be externalized and shared. In that wonderful place, something that I thought I'd been thinking alone took on an external, material, and communal form that was simultaneously philosophical, aesthetic, and political. It wasn't a book written in the void, a prisoner in my mind, mere ink on paper that would turn to dust and vanish into oblivion.

I've often returned to that place. I've written a lot and made many of my current friends there. I've felt a kind of friendship and intellectual affinity that was connected not just with individuals but also with communal life.

Those are all friends who are my equals. But there are some friendships that also have a hierarchy! I think that's the case for all intellectuals. The first people who come to mind are the professors who've become my friends while I've still, in a way, remained their student. I'm thinking of Quentin Meillassoux, Alain Badiou, Francis Wolff, and Sandra Laugier. In my mental theater, they are my interlocutors, and they take me to task when I fail to respond to a position that they embody for me. Sometimes, I feel my thinking become bloated and carried away by an idea. It can take on a heroic – or even a virile – posture as it forgets ordinary things and the solid ground of real, everyday experiences. It's in those moments that I always hear Sandra's voice, which comes from the second Wittgenstein and the American pragmatism of Stanley Cavell, Cora Diamond, and Martha Nussbaum. This voice reminds me of the "uncanny" of the ordinary, of what's already here despite the fact that thinking disregards or forgets it in its rush to embrace the transcendental or the absolute. Whenever I throw myself into theoretical constructions without first analyzing my terms and reexamining the meaning of my concepts, I hear Francis's voice. His Aristotelianism, Cartesianism, and classical way of engaging in analysis and synthesis tell me that I've philosophized poorly – and I know it. If I become bogged down in the details of an investigation, go off course, and lose track of the idea, then I hear Alain's voice decrying the "nitpicking" of the empirical. "Where is the idea?" he asks, "Where is truth?" And, as a general rule, whenever too much of the real makes me lose sight of the possible, I hear Quentin repeating that the object of speculation resides in the "may be." That "may be" is the only thing that makes philosophy worthwhile.

I've always tried to find my line of thinking in the midst of this roundtable of voices and their reminders and calls to order.

And then, of course, there are also the students, since I too have become a teacher. In these cases, the hierarchy is flipped. Those friendships are very gradual and timid, at least at my end. This is because my top priority as a teacher is always to keep their best interest at heart, and to help them succeed, whether they're preparing for entrance exams or going into research. I don't want to disturb them with discussions that falsely present us as on the same footing. I've always hated teachers who feign an informal camaraderie in order to appear cool. That does a real disservice to students by masking its reinforcement of power and domination in a way that eventually makes students feel guilty or betrayed. Within the institutional space, there are simply roles that we play. I don't pretend to be friends with students even if I hope that we might become friends someday. I think that, even though I'm a caring teacher, I can come off as a bit cold at first, partly due to my own shyness.

Over time, some of my former students have become good friends. I'm relieved to not have to be their professor anymore. That's in the past. I'm happy to have had a chance to watch them grow. Some of them have impacted my way of thinking, and in their company, I've come to better understand new ideas that I'd previously only seen from a distance.

All of the courses that I taught in Amiens and then in Lyon have fed my works. I make a point to never give courses based on what I'm thinking or writing. Otherwise, I would be taking advantage of the courses and my students by using my authority to impose something of my way of thinking on them. Nevertheless, the research that I do in preparation for those courses and sometimes with the students in class gives me the material that I use to write books. This was the case for *The Life Intense*, *We Ourselves*, some texts on comedy, others on cultural appropriation, etc. So, I'm the one who's indebted to them, and I thank them for this.

Finally, there's a more melancholic matter. Many friends with whom I have thought have later become estranged for philosophical reasons. Friendships are born, they live, and sometimes they die. When I was younger, there were often moments when someone with whom I'd learned or somehow shared my philosophical education later arrived at a kind of crossroads during a sort of existential crisis. They'd discovered the social sciences, information science and communications, or cognitive science. Then, with that fervor of a new convert, my friend would no longer understand why I was still stuck in the rut of philosophy, an abstract discipline that served no purpose. They would wonder why I was still in a field that had no empirical studies or research laboratories, a solitary field with methods that were rather artistic. Whenever that happened, my heart would always break a little bit. I would wonder if they were the ones who were pulling away or if I was the one going in a different direction. Which of the two of us was remaining true to what had first brought us to theory? Was it complacency or cowardice that kept me hanging on to this old way of thinking? We would still be friendly, but our discussions became increasingly difficult and sometimes even painful. I would feel like I was reliving that long scene in Joyce's *Finnegans Wake* where Shem and Shaun, the two twins, talk to each other from across the river Liffey, which is represented on the book's pages by a column of words flowing through it. As night falls, the river swells, and their words are lost between the rising waters. They can't understand each other any longer, and they mistake one word for another.

What, then, does it feel like I've lost?

I think it's a kind of paradise. Friendship is the only paradise among humans. It's in friendship that, if only for a moment, from across different sides of bodies and words, we understand each other.

PROGRESS AND
MOVEMENT

The political concept of "progressivism" has long been used to structure the political space and to mobilize citizens with the belief in a brighter tomorrow. The notion of progress seems to be in crisis today. It lacks a clear, common definition. Other points of controversy have also appeared within various scientific fields surrounding the criteria used to measure progress, be it real or fake. Do you find progress to be a stimulating political concept? Does it give us a horizon or is it merely an illusion?

For a long time, when I wasn't quite sure how to name my camp, I called myself a "progressive."

At that time, I envisioned progress in emancipation, equality, and individual freedom, as well as in medicine and technology. I thought I was taking the position of a sort of honest modern person.

At the same time, like many in my generation, I had a growing, gnawing feeling, a bitter aftertaste that followed another story, resulting from ecological consciousness in particular, that cast human progress in a different light. Just as Francis Bacon and the Encyclopedists once dreamed, knowledge and technology forged ahead, hand in hand. However, this caused resources to dwindle. In order to power this engine propelling us forward, we harvested from a finite universe that our exploitation was ruining. Where were we even trying to go? Were we aiming for a transhumanist utopia and human enhancement? What about a new generation of phones, an artificial womb, neural implants, robot slaves, or regenerative medicine? Did I really want this bad science fiction image of the future that was supposed to be undeniable? Did I like the image I was being sold of a future that would lead to a California start-up, one of Elon Musk's projects, or the Chinese military–industrial complex? Eventually, I stopped believing in that vision, but I also didn't adopt the belief that I shouldn't believe in progress. I had no desire to become a reactionary. I couldn't see anything desirable about the past or the discourses about it forwarded by those who wanted to keep the world just as it was when it all belonged entirely to them.

In a word, I was hesitant and reluctant. I was really a coward, both in my adherence and in my doubts regarding the idea of progress. Therefore, my position was never very clear.

That changed.

I remember the first discussions that I had in the early 2000s with a group of friends. They were excited about what they'd been reading in English from thinkers in evolutionary psychology that I still knew absolutely nothing about, thinkers like Steven Pinker. He was already known in the United States but not in France. My responses to them were mostly constructionist. Society doesn't have a "nature." Social facts are constructed. To me, attempts to explain a social phenomenon with invariable features that can be naturalized or biologized through an appeal to natural or sexual selection seemed to instantiate a right-wing discourse aimed at legitimating the current order of things. In that discourse, it's natural that things are the way they are, and they should never change. At first, I was caught off guard and thrown off balance by this new discourse of "evopsychology." It was attempting to understand gender differences, inequalities, and social violence through evolutionary phenomena that were both natural and changing. It was a rationalism, a progressivism, and, more than anything else, a kind of optimism that went against the Marxist and critical traditions that had shaped my leftist mind.

That discourse is now widespread. It's been recognized and is now involved in the culture wars. Evolutionary psychology has launched a frontal assault on critiques parsed in terms of social justice, intersectionality, etc. But that was not yet the case.

I wondered if that discourse could be the solution to my indecisiveness. I had become an old, outdated progressive who could only imagine progress in historical terms, like another empire enclosed within that of nature and fenced off from its surroundings. However, within evolutionary psychology, real progress was an *evolution*. It was nothing more than a small measure of movement within living species. It pertained to intraspecific differentiation, competition, and cooperation as well as reproduction between the individuals of a species and the mutations and adaptations of our species. This allowed me to adopt a disengaged, objective viewpoint that wasn't limited to the present where I'd been shortsightedly seeking indications of progress or regression.

During that time, I was most troubled by the initial arguments that I heard regarding the declining trend of violence in human societies. Pinker later wrote a well-known, controversial book on that subject. I think that was really at the heart of the problem. At first, there was a sense of shock and revelation. It seemed like facts, charts, and statistics could refute the worrying feeling that violence was rising and inequality was becoming increasingly ingrained. I wondered if I was just another person who'd given in to the subjective illusion that everything was getting worse because I couldn't see the long-term, objective, and irrefutable trend.

However, I soon had two misgivings about that argument. First, there was the problem that's now at the heart of today's debates surrounding this issue: the discourse of evolutionary psychology caused "violence," "inequality," and "domination" to be split into two parts. The strictly objective part was based on facts and figures, and the other, strictly subjective part was based on feelings and subjective perceptions. The second problem involved measurements: the objective part always entailed measurements, but those measurements came with warnings about their limited applicability due to their origins in statistical studies that were often incomplete. Those same statistics often came out of institutions that rarely qualify as innocent. They have their own interests and biases, and the data that they use is also always incomplete. All of these attempts to measure clearly indicated that something needed to be *defined*. And it's then, at the moment of definition, that the philosophical stakes are at their highest.

In fact, this is precisely the work of thinking. What do we mean by "violence"? What's the strict definition of physical violence? Does there have to be bloodshed for physical violence to have occurred? How is "rape" to be defined? The philosophical moment occurs when we ask these kinds of questions. Relying solely on legal definitions would mean seeing the law as capable of giving us a pure, almost natural, definition of the facts. But laws are just the result of power dynamics. They're tied to specific moments in history. What's defined as "rape," and as "violence" more broadly, changes over time.

That ended my brief fascination with what I would call "evolutionary optimism." This is a belief that the rational, objective mind can produce a science that can periodically rid itself of its prejudices. It would thereby be able to think about what we are and what we do as the results or effects of processes that gradually modify our species and genome under the pressures created by environmental constraints. That's not entirely wrong, and it can often be done well when supplemented with the notion of cultural evolution. Nevertheless, under-standing what we're becoming solely from this point of view produces a mind that believes itself to be lucid, but, sooner or later, it becomes blind to what it defines and discusses as well as to the effects that it has. This rationalism's strictly evolutionary way of conceiving the facts about our species and what we do has effects that prevent me from believing in this kind of evolutionary optimism. That optimism takes on prophetic tones in the work of Yuval Noah Harari. He has found a recep-tive audience among rich philanthropists and others who think of themselves as our humanity's kindhearted parents. They believe they watch over humanity and help it move in the direction of progress.

When we return to the question of progress, we find that something is amiss. First of all, we can only talk about the progress *of something*. That kind of progress is local and determinate, since all that can be measured is the progression of a duration (e.g. the prolongation of life expectancy), a quantity (e.g. purchasing power or average salary), or the repetition of an act (e.g. rapes, violent crimes, thefts, or murders). In this way, it vaguely measures the progress of a value or idea. And yet, the progress of any thing entails a regression with respect to another. The same change can provoke both regret and enthusiasm, or both nostalgia and joy, in equal measure. Even evoking the progress in life expectancy and the prospect of a longer life doesn't mean absolute progress. It can also arouse regrets stemming from missing a life that's shorter and, for that reason, more condensed, uncertain, and intense. This is how we produce an anti-modern, melancholic discourse about how life becomes softer as it grows longer and how it decreases in intensity as it increases in quantity. This discourse emerges in Edmund Burke's thought. As one of the first great reactionary minds, he critiques the drowsiness of our nerves and sees in the aesthetic Sublime a rare hope of overcoming that slumber.

This can certainly be felt today. We make progress with vaccinations and then, in short order, there's a reaction and a feeling that someone or something (like the pharmaceutical industry) is trying to impose change on us by affecting our bodies that once knew how to take care of themselves. This is the anti-vax discourse. All progress produces a reaction, because it's only ever the progress of one thing in particular. This means that progress makes more and more people seek out what has been lost, the price paid for what has been gained. It's like the image that Herder deploys in his critique of the Enlightenment: the ship of history has to jettison weight off the stern in order to move forward. Have we gained more peace and less armed conflict? If so, then we mourn the loss of humanity's heroic era and the virtues of combat. We despise the progress that ushered in the age of commerce and the petty, calculating morality that has replaced the pursuit of glory.

We move forward in one regard, and we move backward in another. We think that our progress is borne out by the facts, but it makes more and more of us melancholic, bitter, and frustrated.

If we still want to be rationalists, then we have no choice but to divide the facts in two: there's objective progress on one side and subjective feeling on the other. This is what we see in today's discussions on topics like immigration or violence. Some people present "objective figures," which others contest with "perceptions within a population." Those discussions lead to a war between the partisans of objectivity and those who champion the truth of feeling. This is what happens when we think that we've presented the human mind with an *unquestionable* idea of progress.

This poisons both our thinking and our lives.

People in one camp will start believing statistics as if they were facts with an authority that's simply beyond some biased people's ability to comprehend. They'll think that others are controlled by their emotions and interests. Those in the other camp will instead fetishize the way that people feel. They'll give our experiences the full weight of truth, even though our vision is always partial – in both senses of the word – and fueled by discourses and images that impact the way that we feel at least as much as our own experiences do. People who feel like violence is rising will talk a little about what they've seen, what they've heard in the street or in the neighborhood, and snippets of conversations they've had with their neighbors, friends, and coworkers. They'll talk a lot more about what they've read, heard on television, seen in newspapers and online, etc.

Unfortunately, the idea of progress leads to fetishization. This is the case with facts that are supposed to be separate from anything subjective, and this is also the case with a pure subjective feeling that's supposed to be unadulterated by images or discourses.

No matter what kind of progress is up for debate, the discussion always ends in the same way: "People are leading longer, healthier lives! Just look at the mortality rate in Europe over the last 300 years. And the same goes for Asia, for Africa, everywhere." To this, the other camp responds: "That may be, but is humanity any happier now? I think that life was better back then."

At the end of the day, any discussion about a form of progress always concludes with a poor and inevitably biased attempt to choose between the data (data about what? How have we defined whatever we're supposedly measuring in terms of progress or regression? Who defined it in that way, and what led them to choose one definition over another?) and the truth of personal feelings.

This is why I always find it misleading to define political categories with terms like "progressive," "conservative," and "reactionary." Even when I'm among friends, I start to feel uncomfortable whenever we discuss "the current state of capitalism." Whether we're talking about this in terms of progress or a capitalist collapse, what do we mean by capitalism? Do we mean capitalism as defined by Marx, Weber, or Sombart? Do we mean the accumulation of investment income, interest-bearing loans, trading companies, systematic accounting, the measurement of economic flows, and the mechanization of society? Do we mean finance capitalism? Or perhaps industrial capitalism? Are we talking about the merchant capitalism that the Hanseatic League spread across northern Europe? How far back should we go? Are we only talking about Europe? What about how the formation of empires relied on administrative rationalization and the levying of taxes? Should we also bring up city-states? What about Babylon and Ur? Some of my autonomist friends trace the enemy that they call "capitalism" all the way back to Neolithic animal domestication, a historical wrong turn that our species took.

That is why, when we talk about movements like progress, regression, evolution, or collapse, I'm never really sure about the *of what* of these movements.

And there's also the question of *whose* movement. Are they the downwardly mobile Europeans or the growing Chinese middle class whose wealth is still increasing? Are they the young people from West Africa who are leaving their countries? Or are they the Amazonian peoples whose way of life has been destroyed?

In any case, any apparent progress also prompts the feeling that it's making something else decrease and eventually disappear. When a neighborhood is renovated, the people who remember how it used to be miss the streets, buildings, and shops that have vanished.

Progress is humiliating. We might think that feeling will pass within a generation, but no, nostalgia leaves a lasting impression on a family's history. The feeling that something has been lost is passed down just as much as the sometimes forced recognition that something has been gained.

I'm opposed to the idea of progress and its philosophical, moral, and political effects for all of these reasons. It's *disorienting*. I would rather think in terms of "movement." When we think that something is progressing, it's better to visualize it as, indeed, "progressing," but in the way that a person progresses when they're venturing out on foot in another country. There's not necessarily an end in mind and, even if there is one, there's nothing to tell us if that end is a good one. The end could also change. All we know is that the person is moving. Their landscape changes as they draw closer to some places and drift farther from others.

Our consciousness is no different: it never progresses toward one thing without becoming more distant from something else. As we gain in experience, we lose in innocence. What matters is the way that we move between experience and innocence. It's like a game of shadows. If there's only one source of light, then it's impossible to shine it on a three-dimensional object without also casting a shadow. When we progress toward a clear knowledge of one side of things, we also plunge the other side into darkness. We can never gain a better understanding from one viewpoint without losing something of what we could see from another. It's all a matter of how we play the game of shadows. We have to decide what we want to bring to light and what we want to leave in the dark.

In this way, when we think about widespread ownership of mobile phones within the last twenty years, I think that we can intuitively understand that this is a matter neither of purely technological progress nor of anthropological regression. It is instead a *movement*. For example, when it comes to social justice, I think it's undeniable that the ability to film everywhere and at all times has allowed people to make visible forms of violence and domination that were formerly only recounted verbally. Even when they were told about, they were only rarely believed. But, in this same movement, we can also clearly see that the flood of images and data makes it much easier to follow, identify, and control people. It's the exact same change that simultaneously weakens and reinforces social control. Beings are thus liberated and imprisoned by the same thing. From this point of view, all talk about the progress or regression of our freedoms seems to be in vain. It's simply more appropriate to discuss how their movement is affected by this technology.

THE WORLD AFTER

Ever since the beginning of the Covid-19 pandemic, there have been many speculations about "the world after," from casual conversations to academics' opinion columns. Aside from the inefficacy that so much repetition can incur, what do you make of that "after"? What do you expect to come after? What do you think that we, along with you, can hope for from what comes next?

My generation's position in history is characterized by endings. I was born with the impression, or the illusion, of having arrived *just after the end of history.* However, as I grew up and even as I grow older, I feel like I've arrived here *just before the end of the world.*

My education coincided with the defeat of the communist bloc, the fall of the Berlin Wall, and the end of the Cold War and bilateral relations. At that time, the air was full of discourses evoking the end of "ideologies" and "grand narratives," the "disenchantment of the world," the defeat of communism, and the rise of a world that was freed from conflict, for better or worse, and handed over to the absolute supremacy of liberal democracy, the ultimate form of politics. I'd arrived too late. History had already played itself out.

In my twenties, I stepped into a new, oppressive fog of images and ideas about climate change, exhausted resources, the Club of Rome's pessimistic recommendations against growth, deteriorating modes of production and governance, the breakdown of state apparatuses, survival horizons, postapocalyptic fictions, zombies, and stories about nature defending itself and reclaiming its rights.

These were all stories. Though not necessarily fables, they were something that we told ourselves.

Progressives loved to think about themselves as being at the end of history, proudly taking their positions as the tip of the spear. Like them, we at least want to believe that we're more than just another link in the chain of history's breakdown. We want to believe that we're the old world's last generation and the first generation to see the "world after." We love bringing about endings. We love slicing world history into two pieces and positioning ourselves squarely between them. This is a form of historical narcissism common to all cultures that showcase and overemphasize their own history. This is what happens to peoples who live in the kind of "hot chronologies" that Lévi-Strauss discusses in *The Savage Mind*. However, this collective psychological impulse is also a means of governance. Pierre Dardot and Christian Laval call this "governing by crisis."

It isn't at all desired or planned, but there always has to be a feeling that someone is in charge. At least when it comes to Western societies, that atmosphere of governance is imbued with a permanent feeling of semi-asphyxia, like we just inhaled a final breath of air or drank a last gulp of water. This makes it constantly feel like we've reached a limit, so we should prepare ourselves, panic (or not), and bounce from one emergency to another, month after month, from climate crisis to health crisis, etc. Governments operate on a cliff's edge. I think that's where those who govern are made.

This is the kind of oppressive atmosphere in which Europe has lived in recent years. The non-stop twenty-four-hour televised news networks illustrate this perfectly. They broadcast dozens of crises and critical moments when "everything is about to be overturned," but nothing is ever really decided. First, there was the Greek bankruptcy and nights spent following the events in Athens, the European troika and its ultimatums, and the Greek government's postponements. Every night, we told ourselves the same thing: "That's it, it's happening today. Greece will have withdrawn from the Eurozone and broken away for good by the time we wake up tomorrow." But no. Possibly for the first time, we instead experienced the almost infinite dilation of a moment that was supposed to be decisive. That dilation actually camouflaged and hid the decision so that it seemed to never have taken place. The same thing happened with Catalonian independence. We came closer and closer to the decisive moment when something irreversible would happen within the autonomous community's parliament, as it was on the verge of becoming a republic. As this decision hung between a yes and a no, it sank in a legal quagmire, and people settled in. The waiting became increasingly wearisome as opaque backroom negotiations took place. Finally, they set up camp and raised the flag right there, on the

edge of the abyss, for years. When the yellow vest movement was at its height in the first autumn in Paris, there
was a similar feeling. Some exhilarated activists even
thought they would storm the Élysée Palace and depose
Emmanuel Macron. In reality, the protests, repression,
broken windows, charges into enemy lines, tear gas,
videos of journalists "reporting live from the heart of
the action," and indignant tweets (here I'm thinking of
Laurent de Sutter's critique of indignation as a political
category) all became ritualistic. Some would even say
they became folklore. Instead of the initial impression
of a five-act tragedy that would take place over five
decisive Saturdays, the acts multiplied into thirty, forty,
fifty, and so on.

Even if Boris Johnson's government seems to be
speeding up the process as I write this, the saga of Brexit
and the United Kingdom's exit from the European
Union is another example of this same kind of event
that is both hystericized and sprawling, with its seem-
ingly endless delays. These events can be drawn out
over weeks or years, testing everyone's patience. Two
more examples here come to mind: the political crisis in
Belgium and the interminable counting of days without
a government, and Hong Kong's Umbrella Movement,
which saw the unprecedented occupation of Hong Kong
Polytechnic University, the fear of an invasion, and the
wait before the state's reassertion of power.

It's also within that context that we should consider
the current Covid-19 epidemic and the call, first made
by activists, then by journalists, and soon thereafter
by institutions, to "think about the world after." This
demonstrates an urgent desire to be done with this and
begin again. At the same time, this call to break away

seems to be eternal. This is like what happens to some couples who spend years talking about a divorce that never comes. They argue and argue until the very idea of separating becomes the only way they can stay together and live from day to day.

Talking about "the world after" quickly came to signify continuing to do things just as we did them before: writing opinion columns for newspapers, collectively organizing symposiums, continuing to try to finally bring things to an end, proposing participatory initiatives, finding slogans, denouncing things online, etc. There was nothing new in that desire for a "new world."

And yet, rather than propelling us into a radically new way of thinking, it seems to me that the Covid-19 epidemic had instead sent us back to a former way of seeing things that we thought was behind us. In a world subjected to cycling pandemics, temporality is more cyclical than linear. So, rather than a break, it's a return. It's the cyclical time that belongs to influenzas and the other large-scale pandemics that affect millions of people almost every century. Even though the Hong Kong flu killed a million people a mere fifty or so years ago, it strangely wasn't preserved in our history and collective memory (although it's now coming back to us). We find it easier to remember things like wars and elections as milestones and breaking points.

Rather than signaling something that's coming, pandemics indicate that something is coming back.

Of course, Covid-19 does have something to tell us about our current state, especially concerning the globalization of trade. However, it presents that globalization as an illness experienced by different populations.

And yet, there's nothing inherently innovative about this. It would be rather odd if we thought that a pandemic would make us change our systems by, for example, breaking with modern capitalism. This would be odd because slavery, two world wars, and ecological devastation have all failed to make us "aware of the problem." Everyone is aware of the problem. Nevertheless, it's clear that no one agrees about the world after. The world after what? What precisely are we talking about here?

In order for there to be a before and an after, there also has to be a *break*. The current pandemic doesn't break with anything. It just erodes certain structures that were already fragile by quickening the spread of corrosion and further weighing down burdens that were already buckling the social body.

That's why I think that the epidemic doesn't have much to do with the category of "event." It isn't a break in continuity or a violent breakthrough of truth, to use Badiou's terms. Rather than something that arrives and breaks time in two, the epidemic rises and falls. So, I believe that we would do better to think about its effects on us in terms of *continuity* instead of *discontinuity*. The epidemic inflects and accentuates. It inflects public policy, opinions, feelings, fears, and fatigue. It accentuates processes of breakdown and decomposition.

For example, when it comes to labor in Western countries, or at least in France, the epidemic accentuates the difference that now appears in the form of new white-collar workers whose jobs require more qualifications and are computer-based. These people can work online and remotely. This isn't just about the service industry or a certain level of professional qualifications, though. It entails measuring the opposition between the kind of job that can be done remotely, from home, and in-person work that requires bodily presence. This presence can involve muscular exertion, but it also includes being in a place or places and subjecting oneself to the materiality of things. People who make deliveries for "services" like Uber Eats and Deliveroo are the prototype for this sort of in-person work that can't be done remotely. This is also the case for chauffeurs, security guards, maintenance staff, and nurses. Teachers, including myself, belong to an intermediate category with its own hierarchy. Preschool and primary-school teachers are required to do their job in person, in sometimes difficult conditions, in order to take care of the children who would otherwise prevent their parents from doing their jobs. However, high-school and university-level teachers like myself are more readily allowed to transition to remote teaching.

Another transformation that's becoming increasingly accentuated is in entertainment, leisure, and consumption broadly construed. Covid-19 has made in-person culture a luxury while reinforcing the broadening market for remote access to cultural events. This can be seen in Amazon's triumph over bookstores and libraries, which will now only survive thanks to a select, elitist, and deliberate audience that supports "cultural agents." It can also be seen in the crowning of Netflix and streamed online fictions as victors over movie theaters and performance spaces. This accentuation is visible in the downtown areas of medium-sized towns as they become increasingly deserted and dilapidated. This process is turning places like Béziers, Tarbes, Châtellerault, and Forbach into ghost towns. The pandemic is not the original source of these changes, but it does reinforce them. It takes what was already strengthening and makes it even stronger, and it further weakens what was already weakening.

What are we to make of that accentuation? I might be mistaken, because it's like using your finger to see where the wind is blowing, but I think that, generally speaking, we're witnessing the movement from liberalism to an authoritarian liberalism. The latter focuses on maintaining order, sovereign authority, control over identity and movement, and data collection. Such an authoritarian liberalism is concerned with managing living spaces. We could almost even call it a model for "carceral liberalism." At least, that's how it comes to be felt by us, the population. In carceral liberalism, our lives seem to imprison us. This especially includes the parts of our lives that are presented to us as pertaining to our freedom. Everything appears more clearly to us when we see it as structures of domination.

The disparities effected by the epidemic that reveal the inequalities between groups are being accentuated. I think that the epidemic also reinforces what has been described as the "Holy Trinity" of contemporary critical thinking: class, gender, and race. Even critical self-analysis of the population's subjugation to the effects of the pandemic still passes through this triple interpretative framework.

In general terms, what's accentuated in the current situation is the desire for a permanent diagnosis of what we're undergoing. By treating our current condition as if it were an illness, each of us becomes a social pathologist in our confinement.

This further accentuates the effects of recent years. Because our time appears to be in crisis, everyone must become a critic of this crisis. With social media, we've seen not only the democratization but also the atomization of the critique that has become a way of life within the liberal regime of contemporary capitalism. Everyone wants their general critical assessment of our situation to be heard by all.

With the pandemic, all conscious individuals have become diagnosticians of what we're all experiencing – which is precisely what I'm doing here. And yet, these diagnoses depend on data that's mainly found online. Those who once had a monopoly on that kind of information now experience disordered democratization as the emergence of "confusionism" or "conspiracism." This is often true, but it also reveals the loss of the "elite's" monopoly over the stories about our lives. This has led to the popularization of diagnoses for our world that we transmit from our homes. I also believe that this sets the stage for a confrontation between who we are at home and who we are in the world that simultaneously makes us strong and weak. When at home, individuals protect themselves, receive data about the world, process it, and then broadcast their diagnosis and judgments about the situation in general.

In a carceral or semi-carceral form of liberalism, the intermediary spaces between the home and the world disappear. We lose the little worlds and common places, the spaces permeated with informal socialization. This liberalism's first priority is to form hermetically sealed bubbles. Those bubbles already existed, but it reinforces them and makes them more visible in order to regulate anything that moves between the inside and the outside. Here we might think of different practices surrounding high-profile sporting events. For example, "protective bubbles" were utilized during the NBA playoffs and the UEFA Champions League finals. Some hyper-secure places test everyone on a regular basis, and others provide rich athletes with everything they need like their transportation, food, and amenities with the requirement that they stay home. From home, they engage with their fans through mediating applications by posting their statuses. We might also think about the private suburbs for the superrich retired people in Florida as well as the Chinese places of power, the neighborhoods exclusively reserved for the highest officials in the Communist Party. This is how some of the upper echelon experience carceral liberalism. The lower versions are found elsewhere, in other neighborhoods like projects and low-income housing blocks. These other versions are also found in extremely tight quarters like studio apartments and the apartments that impoverished students share. Nevertheless, most of those who inhabit these dwellings still have digital access to images of the world and social media accounts.

Confinement has made a certain situation of the self, a form of life, and a mode of existence that seemed to be latent in many people into a literal reality. The result is a number of freedoms, like the freedom to consume and the freedom to express oneself, that are nonetheless bound up with feelings of helplessness, isolation, and house arrest.

People are simultaneously free and imprisoned, in equal measure.

This prison is relative – it allows for temporary release, and it's still partially metaphorical. It becomes a condition for freedom, comfort, protection, delivery of goods, information, images, the daily expression of our state of mind, communication with our loved ones, and the sharing of videos and messages. When mixed together with the fictions of images (especially TV series), ideas, and discourses, reality resembles a vast outside from which our sealed homes provide partial protection, just as they also protect us from the pandemic. And yet, just like the pandemic, the real world threatens to invade our bodies and make us feel the effects of the external reality that we express and share online. We can feel those effects of domination, humiliation, and revolt rising in our bodies as if they were a fever.

The following image is somewhat exaggerated. But it might well give us an idea of how the world has been inflected and accentuated by the current pandemic.

Within living conditions that are equally carceral and liberal, we find some privileged populations who can work remotely and enjoy leisure and cultural activities in person, while other underprivileged populations have to be present at work and access leisure and culture remotely. In accordance with the advantages and disadvantages of their class, race, and gender, those populations organize their lives as a confrontation between their home (an extension of their body) and the world (a system of powers, resources, and images). Their first struggle is to take the diagnosis that they formulate at home and impose it on the world. From their home, the individual takes on the role of a critic with regard to this world viewed as a crisis. In this way, each individual actively participates in the formation of an image of the world in which they feel like a prisoner.

From this constant stream of crises emerges the image of a world that is perpetually "on the verge of collapse." It bathes our minds in a fount of crises and critiques, but it's also a flow that tends toward immobility. This reminds me of the freeze-frame effect that's sometimes used at the beginning or end of movies to give an image of halted, suspended movement (for example, in Robert Aldrich's *The Flight of the Phoenix* or Sam Peckinpah's *The Wild Bunch*). These suspended events are felt by those who govern as well as those who feel governed. We share this atmosphere. And maybe something really is going to happen in the months and years to come. I don't know. In any case, the feeling that something-but-we-don't-know-exactly-what is going to break and that "everything" is just about to collapse is precisely what governs us in the present moment.

The current rhetoric about "the world after" only plays into that atmosphere. It produces a sense of semi-asphyxia as we hang on the edge of an eternally prolonged, frozen collapse. Our current political moment makes us hold our breath, and it also takes our breath away.

That asphyxia fundamentally comes from an increasing scarcity of possibilities. We have to manage the few possibilities that remain according to the demands of the moment. "Now! It's now or never!" And yet, that "now" lasts for a long time. It becomes an age. This age leaves itself and us breathless.

In general, that's how I feel about the age in which we live. Like all feelings, it's undoubtedly exaggerated, and, like those of anyone else, it comes from a specific place. But perhaps others share this feeling with me.

THINKING SAVES

Without pushing you to affirm that thinking saves (although you have suggested as much in the course of our conversation by saying it has made you "happy"), I would love to know some of the "things" that might help us live a little bit better today. There are books, of course, but what else is there, beyond the space of thought, that fulfills and moves you?

I've never had religious feelings – nor, for that matter, irreligious ones. Those feelings are just foreign to me.

Nevertheless, I believe that I understand the idea of salvation. To me, it has always seemed like the horizon of thinking. In my understanding, salvation has nothing to do with the eternal safeguarding of human souls or their access to a paradise. Instead, it involves the always temporary preservation that thought affords to a being's possibility. What is it that damns a being? From what should it be saved? I think that there are two abysses in which we lose things: forgetfulness and identification. By forgetting, a being plunges into a sort of nothingness.

It is no longer anything. It can't even be nothing because it would have to be a thing in order to be nothing. Therefore, saving something means remembering that it isn't nothing or, better yet, not making anything into nothing in the first place. Saving means recognizing that there's always something or someone. However, it's just as damning to be forced into a finite, definitive form and to be identified once and for all. "There, that's what it is!" "There, that's what you are!" Identification reduces whatever something might be to just a part of what it is, or even all that it currently is, in a way that prevents it from ever being able to become something else. It becomes a that, and nothing more than that. To save a being is to return its possibility to it. Saving it allows it to be one way or another and therefore to become something else. At the same time, saving a being restores its power.

This salvation is the complete opposite of this age's feeling of asphyxia. Thinking makes things possible. It lets us imagine how what there is might be different. It allows us to see difference and that there's time for things to become different.

Rather than leading us into eternity, salvation takes us into time.

This very clearly matters for those around us. Our judgments of other men and women constantly cast them into a nothingness that has neither past nor present. We forget about them, make them invisible, and behave as if they never existed. From this point of view, history is the most destructive power. It treats people as if they had never been and could never become anything else, and in doing so it generates an ever-growing mass of nonexistent, anonymous lives. When it's directed toward the past, thinking retrieves something from everything that has ever been born, grown up, felt, suffered, done or undone acts of good or evil, and passed away. Otherwise, there's amnesia, the hell for all that we've forgotten.

However, thinking also means constantly struggling to avoid judgments that reduce a person to what they are. By thinking, we try to preserve each person's power to become something, right up to their death. Everyone does what they can with that power. However, totally stripping someone of that power reduces them to a mere characteristic of themselves. It mistakes them for or conflates them with a fixed image – be it glorious or foul – of their being. This betrays the very power that we're striving to save.

That task extends well beyond our fellow humans. By thinking, we also endeavor to save life, images, and ideas. We try to save whatever they might be able to do for us. And yet, we can never save them once and for all. Things are saved inasmuch as they are thought, but no one thinks eternally, even when we're thinking about eternity. We can just prolong a thing's possibility so that it's preserved for a few hours, days, or years.

If we stop thinking, then there is only what there is. Possibility passes away or, at the very least, we no longer perceive it. Then there is nothing that is either damned or saved. There is, and that's it. But as soon as vegetable, animal, and human beings perceive their environment, what there is and what there is not, what there may be and should be, as soon as they imagine and remember, then everything can be forgotten. Everything can be identified, defined and finished. Or, everything can be saved, which is to say, everything can be made possible and powerful.

That's what I research, and that's what brings me fulfillment. Of course, what I find truly fulfilling – the beings that I love – only concerns me. But I hope for something that also belongs to all of us: a power to save that's not divine but that belongs to everything that lives, feels, perceives, and thinks, even if it's just a little bit.

That might seem like an intellectual construct, but I really do believe in it. My faith as a novelist and philosopher rests in this. For a time, we can *save* things when we give them back their possibility by perceiving them, describing them, conceiving of them, and sheltering them in a living structure of thought.

That's enough for me, and that's how I imagine everything to be. If something isn't anything, or if it's only this way and not any other way, or if it must be a certain way, it's finished. Whenever it can be, it's saved.